DIETRICH BONHOEFFER

Dietrich Bonhoeffer

Called by God

ELIZABETH RAUM

Continuum
New York · London

2002
The Continuum International Publishing Group Inc
370 Lexington Avenue, New York, NY 10017

The Continuum International Publishing Group Ltd
The Tower Building, 11 York Road, London SE1 7NX

Printed in the United States of America

Library of Congress Cataloging-in-Publication Data

Raum, Elizabeth.
    Dietrich Bonhoeffer : called by God : a biography / by
Elizabeth Raum.

        p. cm.
Includes bibliographical references and index.
    ISBN 0-8264-1380-3
    1. Bonhoeffer, Dietrich, 1906-1945.   I. Title
    BX4827.B57 R38 2002
    230'.044'092—dc21

                    2002000376

Grateful acknowledgment is made for permission to reprint text and photographs from the following sources:

All photographs in the book are copyright © Chr. Kaiser/Gütersloher Verlagshaus, Gütersloh, and are reprinted by permission.

Dietrich Bonhoeffer: A Biography (Revised Edition) by Eberhard Bethge, revised and edited by Victoria J. Barnett. Copyright © 2000 HarperCollins. Used by permission of Augsburg-Fortress.

A Testament to Freedom: The Essential Writings of Dietrich Bonhoeffer, edited by Geffrey B. Kelly and F. Burton Nelson. Copyright © 1991 by Geffrey B. Kelly and F. Burton Nelson. Reprinted by permission of HarperCollins Publishers, Inc., and HarperCollins, Ltd., and F. Burton Nelson.

I Knew Dietrich Bonhoeffer by Wolf-Dieter Zimmermann. Copyright © 1967 by William Collins & Sons Company, Ltd., London, and Harper & Row Publishers, Inc., New York. Copyright renewed 1995. Reprinted by permission of HarperCollins Publishers, Inc., and HarperCollins, Ltd.

The Bonhoeffers: Portrait of a Family. Copyright © 1994 Covenant Publications. Reprinted by special permission of Covenant Publications, Chicago, Illinois.

To Rick

———————————————————

"Keep alert, stand firm in your faith, be courageous, be strong. Let all that you do be done in love." (1 Corinthians 16:13 14)

Contents

Acknowledgments

N O AUTHOR TODAY CAN WRITE about Dietrich Bonhoeffer without relying on the pioneering work of Eberhard Bethge. This book, and indeed every book, article, dissertation, or film based on the life and work of Dietrich Bonhoeffer, owes a tremendous debt of gratitude to Eberhard Bethge. In the years immediately after the war, Bethge guided Bonhoeffer's *Ethics* to publication, organized and published Bonhoeffer's letters and papers, and wrote a definitive biography, *Dietrich Bonhoeffer: Man of Vision–Man of Courage*, published first in Germany and then released in the United States by Augsburg Fortress in 1970 on the twenty-fifth anniversary of Bonhoeffer's death. Bethge, often with the assistance of his wife, Renate, edited numerous books and spoke at conferences worldwide on the life and theology of Dietrich Bonhoeffer. He also worked tirelessly to promote an ongoing Christian–Jewish dialogue in the aftermath of the Holocaust, a cause intimately tied to his own interpretation of Bonhoeffer's theological work.

For this author, as for so many others, Eberhard Bethge not only provided original source materials and a unique knowledge of Bonhoeffer but also gentle encouragement. When I first contacted him in 1997, Pastor Bethge replied that despite difficulties reading and writing (he was eighty-eight years old at the time), he would like to see my draft of this manuscript. He read the manuscript, wrote a page of suggested corrections, and encouraged me to continue. A year later when I met the Bethges in their home near Bonn, Germany, I was touched by their continued interest in this project and their willingness to share both their home and their memories with me.

Eberhard Bethge passed the manuscript along to his sister-in-law, Dorothee Bracher, who, like Bethge's wife, Renate, is a niece of Dietrich Bonhoeffer. I thank Ms. Bracher for reading this manuscript in its early stages and providing me with notes and comments that proved essential to the accuracy of this work. The memoirs of Sabine Leibholz-Bonhoeffer, recorded in *The Bonhoeffers: Portrait of a Family* and the reminiscences collected and edited by Wolf-Dieter Zimmermann and Ronald Gregor Smith in *I Knew Dietrich Bonhoeffer: Reminiscences by His Friends* provided me with an intimate and personal portrait of Dietrich as brother, friend, teacher, and pastor.

I also thank the legions of theologians who have analyzed and interpreted the words of Bonhoeffer and the translators who have made his works available to non–German-speaking peoples throughout the world. Particularly I thank Dr. Jonathan Clark of the Concordia College German Department for his translation help, and Pastor Michael Hayes and Dr. Dale Shook for reading through the manuscript in various stages.

I also wish to thank tour leaders Marlan and Sharon Johnson, who provided me with the opportunity to meet Bonhoeffer friends and family in Germany and to visit many of the places that played a role in his life. I thank Hans-Christoph von Hase and his wife, Agnes, Wolf-Dieter Zimmermann, and Ruth-Alice von Bismarck for providing their personal insights into the life of Dietrich Bonhoeffer. In addition, I thank the Faith and Learning Committee of Concordia College, Moorhead, Minnesota, for providing financial support for my trip to Germany.

Finally, I wish to thank my husband, Richard Raum, for first introducing me to the life and work of Dietrich Bonhoeffer and for supporting and encouraging me as I completed this project.

1

The Search for
Dietrich Bonhoeffer

1945

I N MAY 1945 THE CITY OF BERLIN, Germany, lay in ruins. Allied bombs had crumbled buildings and blocked major thoroughfares. Few in the West were sympathetic to the plight of this enemy people, the Germans, who had started the most devastating war in the world's history. For Americans, it was a time of rejoicing. The war was over, soldiers were returning home, and most people felt that the Germans deserved whatever harsh conditions they faced. Few guessed or would have cared that among the people traversing the Berlin streets after the war were heroes, Germans who had stood up to Hitler and struggled against his insidious decrees.

Eberhard Bethge was such a man. He had been arrested by the Gestapo in October of 1944 on suspicion of treason against the state and was imprisoned in Berlin. His trial was scheduled for May 15, 1945, but by then Hitler was dead, the war had ended, and Eberhard joined the thousands of Europeans searching for news of missing family and friends. He rode his bicycle through the bomb-blasted streets of Berlin searching for anyone who might have information about the whereabouts of his closest friend, Dietrich Bonhoeffer. Sometimes Eberhard was forced to stop and lift his bicycle over piles of debris as he made his way from one burned-out government office to the next. After years of constant bombing, the once beautiful Berlin streets were piled high with rubble. Eberhard met other Berliners who wandered aimlessly through the streets looking for food, trying to avoid the marauding Russian soldiers and hoping to locate their loved ones.

The world watched in horror as Allied troops broadcast the news of the Holocaust and its devastation. Thousands of Europeans waited anxiously to learn the fate of family members and friends. Over six million Jews, including one and a half million children, had been ruthlessly slaughtered by the Nazis and buried in unmarked graves. Gypsies, the disabled, homosexuals, and any who dared to oppose Hitler had also been targeted by the Nazis. All tolled, between thirty-five million and sixty million people had lost their lives in the death camps, battlefields, and bombing raids of World War II. How could Eberhard or anyone else find one missing person among so many?

Weeks passed as Eberhard tried to locate someone, perhaps a former prison guard or a fellow prisoner, who could provide even a hint of where Dietrich Bonhoeffer might have been taken. For nearly two years Dietrich had been imprisoned in Berlin, first at the Tegel Prison and then at the Gestapo interrogation prison on Prinz-Albrecht-Strasse. On February 7, Dietrich was secretly transferred out of Berlin, but his family did not discover the move until a week later when they visited the prison and found it deserted. Dietrich's older brother Klaus and his brothers-in-law Hans von Dohnanyi and Rüdiger Schleicher had also been imprisoned by the Gestapo. All three had been sentenced to death. The family hoped that the war would end before the death sentences could be carried out. Letters from the men dated March and April 1945, the last letters to reach the family, spoke openly about their death sentences and the ways in which each had come to terms with his fate. Rüdiger Schleicher wrote to his wife of his gratitude for her love, "which surrounds me at every turn and also strengthens me internally in my existence."[1] Klaus Bonhoeffer wrote to his parents, "On this ride between death and the devil, death is really a noble companion."[2]

For months the Bonhoeffer family had managed to keep in

touch with their men in prison, sending food parcels whenever possible and using whatever influence they could exert to make conditions at least a bit more bearable. They had devised a clever code system that allowed them to send notes back and forth, and after a time, Dietrich had found guards willing to smuggle uncensored letters to his friend Eberhard. Now that the fighting was finally over and Hitler was defeated, the men had vanished. Where were they? What had happened? During that dreary May in 1945 Eberhard searched for them all, these friends who had become family through marriage.[3]

Hopes were dashed on May 31, 1945, when Eberhard Bethge "met a man named H. Kosney near the prison." According to Emmi Bonhoeffer, the wife of Dietrich's brother Klaus, Kosney was

> the only survivor of the sixteen men who were taken to be shot that night. Kosney had been able to turn his head so that he was merely shot in the cheek. He pretended to be dead and later described how he heard the lieutenant say, "Quickly, quickly, gentlemen, we've still got more to do."[4]

Rüdiger Schleicher and Klaus Bonhoeffer were among the men who had been killed by the S.S. executioners over a month earlier on April 22, 1945.

There was still no definite word of Hans von Dohnanyi or Dietrich Bonhoeffer. In April 1945, Christine von Dohnanyi received a note from a doctor at the Sachsenhausen Concentration Camp which implied that her husband had been killed. However, as one family member recalled, "since it was vague, somehow we did not accept it."[5] In June 1945 Karl-Friedrich, Dietrich's oldest brother, wrote to his children who had been evacuated to the Harz Mountains of the family's futile attempt to locate either their Uncle Hans or Uncle Dietrich. Maria von Wedemeyer, Dietrich's fiancée, who had been living in Berlin with the Bonhoeffer parents, had also searched to no avail. Dietrich's youngest sister reported in a videotaped interview that "we kept on hoping that we would have some news about Dietrich. Many people said that they had seen him. I suppose they were just trying to be friendly."[6]

On May 31, 1945, Dietrich's twin sister, Sabine, who was living in England, learned that Dietrich had been murdered by the Nazis at the Flossenbürg Concentration Camp on April 9, 1945. The news had reached England via prisoners who had escaped from Flossenbürg into the hands of American forces in Italy. Word was sent first to church leaders in Geneva and then to Bishop George Bell in England. Bell had been a friend of Dietrich and had helped Sabine and her family relocate to England. It was Bishop Bell who made sure that Sabine received the sad news about the death of her beloved twin brother. Sabine wrote of that day in her memoirs:

> Somehow I had been living wholly for the moment when I could be reunited with Dietrich in a new and better Germany, when we would tell each other our adventures and exchange our news about all that had taken place in these difficult years. Dietrich himself had likewise said in his letters how much he was looking forward to that moment when we would be reunited. Now I felt as though all the lights had been put out."[7]

In the postwar chaos, with the German news media destroyed and communication difficult if not impossible between Germany and England, the family in Berlin remained unaware that Dietrich's death had been confirmed. Eberhard continued his search for information throughout the early summer.

On July 27, 1945, Eberhard and rest of the Bonhoeffer family learned from a neighbor that the BBC was planning to broadcast a memorial service in London for Dietrich Bonhoeffer that very afternoon. That was when they first heard the news they had so long dreaded. The family listened to the radio broadcast as British church leader George Bell, who had become a friend of the young Bonhoeffer years before, said during that service:

> As one of a noble company of martyrs of differing traditions, he [Bonhoeffer] represents both the resistance of the believing soul, in the name of God, to the assault of evil, and also the moral and political revolt of the human conscience against injustice and cruelty. He and his fellows are indeed built upon the foundation of the Apostles and the Prophets.[8]

Shortly after receiving this news Dr. Karl Bonhoeffer, Dietrich's father, wrote to a friend:

> For years we endured the tension, the anxiety about those arrested and those who were not yet arrested but in danger. But since we were all agreed about the necessity of action, and my sons were also fully aware of what they could expect if the plot miscarried, and had resolved if necessary to lay down their lives, we are sad, but also proud of their straight and narrow attitude.[9]

In the years since World War II the world has learned something about the courageous men and women who tried to overthrow Adolf Hitler from inside the Third Reich. There are hundreds of books and dissertations analyzing Dietrich Bonhoeffer's theological works, but for many it is his actions, as well as his words, that have inspired them to make the difficult decision to oppose evil and to live in response to God's call to costly discipleship.

2

Childhood: A Short
and Happy Peace

1906–1916

GERMANY WAS AT PEACE on February 4, 1906, when Dietrich Bonhoeffer was born. His was an idyllic childhood lived in the comfort of a large and loving family. He was the sixth child born to Karl and Paula Bonhoeffer, and his twin sister, Sabine, born ten minutes later, became the seventh. Both of his parents had come from prominent German families whose ancestors included doctors, politicians, and clergymen. His father, Karl Bonhoeffer, attended the medical college at Tübingen, worked in various hospitals, and eventually became a professor of psychiatry and neurology in Breslau, Germany.

It was there in 1896 that he met Paula von Hase, who would become Dietrich's mother. Many years later, Karl Bonhoeffer wrote in his *Memoirs* that he met "a young, fair, blue-eyed girl whose bearing was so free and natural that as soon as she entered the room, she took me captive."[1] Two years later they married. Karl-Friedrich, their first child, was born in 1899, followed in rapid succession by Walter (also born in 1899) and Klaus (1901). Ursula and Christine were born in 1902 and 1903. The twins were born in 1906, and Susanne, the youngest, was born in 1909. Karl and Paula Bonhoeffer provided their children with a love of music, a fondness for intellectual discussion, and lots of time for outdoor play

16

in the German countryside. The Bonhoeffers were delighted with their large family. Dr. Bonhoeffer wrote in his diary in 1909:

> Although eight children seems an extraordinarily large number for these days, we feel that there are not too many of them. The house is roomy, the children have grown up normally, we parents are not too old yet, and are therefore concerned not to spoil them but to make their youth a happy time.[2]

In 1912, when Dietrich was six, his father was appointed professor of psychiatry and neurology at the University of Berlin. The family left Breslau and settled in an area of Berlin called Tiergarten. The Bonhoeffers were well-to-do and therefore were able to afford several servants—a governess, nursemaids, housemaids, and a cook. With its spacious gardens and excess of rooms, the Bonhoeffer house was an ideal playground for the children. The three older boys, Karl-Friedrich, Walter, and Klaus, gathered a large menagerie in their workshop. They had cages for snakes and lizards and a collection of butterflies, beetles, and birds' eggs. The older girls, Ursula and Christine, were given a room of their own where they could keep their dolls. When they were grown, the Bonhoeffer children fondly recalled that they were never punished for tearing their clothes or breaking their toys. They were given the freedom to play as they liked, and their mother loved to surprise them with games, songs, and special parties.

Dietrich's mother, who had taken the unusual step of earning a teaching degree before her marriage, taught the older children herself. However, by the time that Dietrich, Sabine, and Susanne were ready for lessons, their mother was involved in so many other activities that she turned much of the teaching of the younger children over to their governess, Kate Horn.

Fräulein Horn and her sister, Maria, joined the family six months after the twins were born. As the children grew, Kate Horn took over the role of teacher. She reported that "there was never any difficulty with teaching or with their homework. . . . All three were jolly children with whom it was a pleasure to play or to go for walks."[3] The children liked their governess and enjoyed surprising her with small kindnesses, like setting the supper table before she had the chance to do it herself. Fräulein Horn always assumed that Dietrich instigated such plans.

Like all children, Dietrich had a mischievous side. When Kate Horn was asked about her years as governess to the Bonhoeffer children, she recalled that Dietrich tended to misbehave when there was reason to rush to get ready to go out. On one such day, Dietrich

> was dancing round the room, singing and being a thorough nuisance. Suddenly the door opened, his mother descended upon him, boxed his ears right and left, and was gone. Then the nonsense was over. Without shedding a tear, he now did what he ought.[4]

Dietrich formed a warm and loving relationship with Kate Horn. It was Fräulein Horn who was with the children during many of the difficult moments of their childhood. In August of 1914, for example, the Bonhoeffer children were with Kate Horn in the German countryside near Friedrichsbrunn when she heard the news that Germany was at war. She rushed the children back to Berlin to be with their parents.

Despite his busy schedule at the hospital and the university, Karl Bonhoeffer always managed to spend mealtimes with the family. One of the children said grace before each meal. The children were not allowed to speak unless spoken to, were never to discuss the food, and were expected to finish whatever was on their plates. After meals, they were required to be silent so that their parents could take a short nap.

It was not Karl Bonhoeffer's practice to lecture or scold the children. Rather, he taught them by example to speak simply and precisely, to think clearly, to ignore pain, and to do their best work. A childhood friend, Emmi Delbrück, who later married Dietrich's brother Klaus, wrote:

> In the Bonhoeffer family one learnt to think before asking a question or making a remark. It was embarrassing to see their father raise his left eyebrow inquiringly. It was a relief when this was accompanied by a kindly smile, but absolutely devastating when his expression remained serious. But he never really wanted to devastate, and everybody knew it.[5]

As he grew older, Dietrich's friends and colleagues commented on what a good listener he was.

Dietrich eventually outgrew Fräulein Kate's home schooling. In 1913 he enrolled at the Friedrich Werder Grammar School, which his brothers also had attended. Dietrich was an excellent student. In 1915 his father wrote in his diary, "Dietrich does his work naturally and tidily."[6]

It was his father's influence, as well as his mother's, that taught Dietrich to set aside time for music, games, and social evenings with friends. Sometimes on Sunday nights Karl Bonhoeffer would read literary classics to the children. Susanne, the youngest, who was called Susi by her family, remembered her father reading the children a particularly sad passage from a story. "I wept a lot," she wrote, "so my father stopped reading and we had juice and cakes until I was recovered."[7]

Dietrich enjoyed painting and sculpture and reading. His favorite books included *Pinocchio, Heroes of Everyday*, and a translation of Harriet Beecher Stowe's novel about the lives of Southern slaves, *Uncle Tom's Cabin*. Dietrich also liked to read fairy tales and then to act them out with his sisters. A big box of costumes was always available for skits and plays, and the family was more than willing to serve as an audience.

On Saturday evenings the family played music together. Dietrich began piano lessons at age eight. He quickly learned to read music by sight and often accompanied Klaus, who played the cello, Sabine, who played the violin, and Ursula, Christine, or his mother, who sang. Dietrich made such fast progress on the piano that his parents wondered if he might become a professional musician. By the time he was ten he played Mozart's sonatas and even tried his hand at musical composition.

Throughout his life Dietrich turned to music in times of great joy and in times of deep despair. He played the piano at family gatherings and with friends and students. Years later, when he was director of a seminary, he made certain that a piano was available for group singing, and he used music to create community among the students. Later still, when he was a political prisoner in a Gestapo jail and had no piano at hand, the melodies and words of the hymns he knew by heart gave him great comfort and courage.

As the youngest boy, Dietrich spent his childhood years striving to keep up with his older brothers. There was a five-year span between Dietrich and Klaus, however, and that proved to be too big a gap to be easily overcome. Eberhard Bethge, in his classic biography of Bonhoeffer, suggests that Dietrich felt a secret rivalry with his bigger brothers. "It was natural that the sturdy and gifted boy should sometimes try to rival or even surpass his big brothers, and, indeed, in the field of music, he did surpass them."[8]

In later years, Dietrich became particularly close to his brother Klaus and to the husbands of his sisters Christine and Ursula. All four, along with many Bonhoeffer relatives and friends eventually joined in political opposition to Hitler. But as a child, Dietrich spent most of his time in the company of Sabine and little Susi, where he enjoyed his special status as the stronger, more athletic older brother to two sisters. Dietrich inherited his mother's blond hair and sensitive nature, and from his father he learned to use language precisely and to set high standards for himself.

The Bonhoeffers had both a city and a country home. After the move to Berlin when Dietrich was six, they purchased a simple lodge in Friedrichsbrunn in the Harz Mountains. The children often traveled to the country home with their governess, and they were encouraged to bring friends and cousins with them. There the children romped in the woods gathering berries or mushrooms. Dietrich always loved games and liked to win, but he also had a reputation for fairness. In the early evenings the Bonhoeffer children played ball games in the big meadow with the children from the village. Later they all gathered in the Bonhoeffer living room and played guessing games or sang folk songs.

It was in Friedrichsbrunn that Dietrich developed his love of the German countryside. Like his father, he was a keen observer who knew the names of many plants that grew in the German forests. Dietrich always found joy in fresh air and sunshine, and many years later he found ways to bring his confirmation classes and his university students to the country. His teaching assistant, Wolf-Dieter Zimmermann, remembered a visit to Dietrich's mountain cabin in March 1933. As the two men sat outside and watched the stars, Dietrich described each constellation in exquisite detail. "How do you know this?" Zimmermann asked. "One knows," Dietrich said. It was proof to Zimmermann not only of Dietrich's powers of observations, but of his keen intelligence, his thorough education, and his appreciation of the world around him.[9] In a letter written in 1943 when he was in Tegel Prison, Dietrich recalled his days in the woods:

> In my imagination I live a good deal in nature, in the glades near Friedrichsbrunn. . . . I lie on my back in the grass, watch the clouds sailing in the breeze across the blue sky, and listen to the rustling of the woods. . . . It is the hills of central Germany, the Harz, the Thuringian forest, the Weserberge, that to me represent nature . . . and have fashioned me.[10]

Even the journey to Friedrichsbrunn was a delight for Dietrich and Sabine. The children, under the supervision of Fräulein Horn, traveled by train to Thale, then transferred their luggage to two carriages. The girls rode the remaining six kilometers to the house, but the boys often hopped out and hiked along a beautiful path through the forest. On those occasions when their parents came to spend time with the children in the country, the children would place candles in all the windows so that the house glowed with welcome.

Sometimes, when the hustle of the big household became too much, Dietrich would escape to his room. He needed some quiet time alone before he could face the crowd again. Throughout his life, Dietrich drew strength from quiet, meditative moments. As he grew older, he turned to prayer and Scripture reading for such strength. His friends considered him reserved, although they were quick to add that he had a wonderful sense of humor.

As Germany's attention shifted to the battlefields of the First World War a great shadow fell over Dietrich and his family. The parties, the playful family evenings, the sense of safety and security were shattered by enemy bullets. It was at this time, when Dietrich and Sabine were about eight years old, that they began to talk seriously about death. What did it feel like to be dead? As very young children, they had watched funeral processions draw

up to the large Catholic cemetery across from their home in Breslau. Now thoughts of death intruded in a more personal way. Several years later Sabine recalled:

> And so in the evenings after prayers and hymn singing, in which
> our mother always took part when she was in the house, we used
> to lie awake for a long time and try to imagine to ourselves what it
> must be like to be dead and to have entered upon eternal life. We
> used to make special efforts to draw a little nearer every evening to
> eternity by resolving to think only of the word "eternity" and not
> to admit any other thought to our minds. This eternity seemed to
> us very long and uncanny. After concentrating intently for a long
> time our heads often used to swim. We staunchly kept up this self-
> imposed exercise for a long time. We were very dependent upon
> one another and each wanted to be the last to call out the final
> "good night" to the other.[11]

In March of 1916, when Dietrich was ten, the family moved to a
larger house in the Grunewald district of Berlin. The large, comfortable house at 14 Wangenheimstrasse provided lots of room for
gatherings of friends and family. Many professors and their families lived in the neighborhood, and the children quickly befriended
their new neighbors. In fact, several of the Bonhoeffer children
chose their husbands and wives from among the neighboring
families.

The new house also helped the family deal with the severe food
shortages brought on by war. They were able to grow their own
vegetables in the spacious yard, and for a short while longer,
Dietrich, Sabine, and Susanne enjoying playing games there. In
1917, however, when Dietrich was only eleven years old, the war
intruded so violently into the lives of the Bonhoeffers that it
changed them forever. For Dietrich, the darkest days of his childhood were about to begin, but the sound values that governed his
early life provided an anchor for him during the troubled times
ahead.

3

The First Death

WHEN THE FIRST WORLD WAR BEGAN, Dietrich was eight and a half years old. He greeted the war news with enthusiasm. Like many young German boys he plotted the progress of the German troops by sticking colored pins into a map. When he was away from Berlin for a summer holiday in the country, he asked his parents to send him newspaper clippings so that he could keep his map up-to-date. At first, war was fun and games to young Dietrich. His twin sister, Sabine, recalled that

> Dietrich played at "soldiers" in the garden with me, Susi, and our neighbor's son. More drilling was done than shooting; but when a sand bomb was thrown against the hen run and a clucking hen burst forth, such warlike practice was considered mean by Dietrich and prohibited.[1]

After all, the family was depending on the eggs for breakfast.

As the war progressed, food shortages affected even prosperous families like the Bonhoeffers. Dietrich, who was always a good eater, took responsibility for finding out where certain foods could be purchased. He learned the "black market" prices of speciality foods and was able to direct the servants to the shortest lines at the least expensive places. His father found this newfound talent quite amusing, as well as helpful. The gardens behind the house provided extra vegetables, and the chickens and goats produced eggs and milk to supplement the food purchased at the market.

German losses on the battlefield eventually brought the news to Dietrich and his sisters that three older cousins, ages eighteen to twenty years old, had been killed in battle. The fathers of school classmates were reported killed on the front lines. A cousin, blinded at the front, came to live with the Bonhoeffers for a while. War was no longer simple fun and games.

Dietrich was eleven when his two oldest brothers were called up for military service. Both enlisted in the infantry, where soldiers were needed most. When Walter, a quiet, studious boy of eighteen, left for the Western front the entire family joined together for a musical evening, and Dietrich sang Walter a special farewell song. The next day they all accompanied Walter to the train station.

Just two weeks later, on April 23, 1918, Walter was seriously wounded. He died five days later in a field hospital. For Dietrich, death was now a cruel reality rather than an abstract idea. Dietrich inherited the Bible that Walter had been given at confirmation. It became a valued possession and signaled a new direction in Dietrich's life.

Dietrich's closest childhood friend, his cousin Hans-Christoph von Hase, recalled that it was immediately after Walter's death, when Dietrich was twelve, that he decided to study theology, although he didn't announce his decision until much later. The boys, only a year apart in age, had spent time together during family vacations both in Berlin and in the country parish where Hans-Christoph's father served as pastor. They wrote to each other throughout their childhood and during their teenage years, but it was after Walter's death that Hans-Christoph's father began sending packages containing theology books to his young nephew.[2] These included books that had belonged to Dietrich's grandfather, Karl Alfred von Hase, who had been a professor of practical theology in Breslau. Dietrich's great-grandfather was also a theologian, and young Dietrich owned a signed copy of his great-grandfather Karl August von Hase's textbook on the history of dogmatics.

Walter's death had a profound effect on everyone in the family, although Dietrich's decision to study theology was perhaps the most far-reaching. Dietrich's mother, overcome with grief, withdrew from the family and spent several weeks in bed at a neighbor's home. It was difficult for the Bonhoeffer children to see their once strong mother weakened by grief. It was more than a year before Paula Bonhoeffer was able to resume her normal activities.

Walter's death cast a shadow over Dietrich's life that never fully disappeared. In 1930, when Dietrich was twenty-four years old, he preached a sermon titled "On God's Message of Love to Germany and the Community of Nations" to a New York City congregation. When he spoke of Germany as a "house of mourning," he spoke from his own heart, adding that "the same November 11, 1918, which brought to us the end of the war, was the beginning of a new epoch of suffering and grief."[3]

It was in November 1918, when Dietrich was twelve, that a parliamentary government known as the Weimar Republic was formed. The harsh terms of the Versailles Treaty, the unstable economy, and the turmoil of defeat created insurmountable obstacles for the new government. From his classroom in Berlin, Dietrich heard gunshots as Germany exploded in near civil war. Communist factions fought against their opposite, the extreme right-wing movement, and both groups hoped to overthrow the Weimar Republic. Dietrich and his sisters walked to school past soldiers manning barricades and within earshot of the fighting. The unrest in Berlin was eventually quelled by the army, but violence continued in other areas of Germany. As many as one thousand people died in Munich in April of 1919 in the civil unrest. Thousands more nearly starved because of the harsh economic conditions. Dietrich told his American audience:

> I myself was in these years a schoolboy and I can assure you that not only I had in those days to learn what hunger means. . . . Instead of a good meal there was largely sawdust in our bread and

the fixed portion for every day was five or six slices of that kind of bread. . . . The substitute for meat, fish, vegetables, even for coffee, jam and toast—were [*sic*] turnips for breakfast, lunch, and supper.[4]

Small children and old people were especially hard hit by the conditions. The flu epidemic of 1918 claimed the lives of more than one hundred thousand victims. Few had the strength to fight against disease. In such conditions, the suicide rate increased. Dietrich later said,

> I remember very well I had on the way to my school to pass by a bridge and in the winters from 1917 to 1919 almost every morning when I came to this bridge I saw a group of people standing on the river and everybody who passed by knew what had happened. These impressions were hard for young boys.[5]

Like most Germans, Dietrich was appalled by the suffering he saw on the streets of Berlin and by the harsh terms imposed on his country by the Versailles Treaty. The treaty reclaimed much German land, limited Germany's army to one hundred thousand men, deprived Germany of colonies, and prevented Germany from uniting with Austria. In addition, Germany was forced by the "war guilt clause" to accept responsibility for the war and to pay reparations to other nations. As a result, Germans became strong nationalists willing to defend their country at all costs. They were also looking for a scapegoat—someone else to blame for their troubles. Eventually Adolf Hitler seized on a long tradition of anti-Semitism and singled out the Jews as responsible for Germany's economic woes. He used the false notion of racial purity to rally non-Jewish Germans against their Jewish friends and neighbors.

In 1919, however, Hitler had not yet emerged as a prominent German leader. Dietrich, at age thirteen, was a loyal German, devoted to his country and its traditions. He joined the Scouts, an organization of the German Youth Movement which instilled pride in all things German. The Scouts were led by older men, often schoolteachers. On Sunday mornings the boys attended military drills and had mock battles. In the winter Dietrich lent his musical talents to his Scout troop by playing works by such

German composers as Schubert and by arranging Haydn trios for Scout concerts. Dietrich remained a Scout for one year, and then, without explanation, he quit the organization.

Despite the alarming political events in their midst, the Bonhoeffer children continued to enjoy school, games, and music. Sabine and Dietrich took dance lessons and joined neighborhood friends in parties and balls. Dietrich became close friends with Hans Delbrück, whose sister Emmi later married Dietrich's brother Klaus. Another family, the Dohnanyis, joined the social group and eventually became united with the family when Hans von Dohnanyi married Dietrich's sister Christine.

Although he had not formally declared his intention to study theology, Dietrich's mind often wandered to spiritual concerns. His friends liked to ask him theological questions. "Is evil really overcome by good?" or "Should we offer the other cheek to the insolent person, too?" Dietrich often responded by asking another question which forced his friends to think even more deeply. "Do you think Jesus wanted anarchy? Did he not go into the temple with a whip to throw out the money-changers?"[6]

When they were fourteen, Dietrich and Sabine followed local custom and took confirmation classes with Pastor Priebe of the Grunewald Church. Like most German Evangelical churches, the Grunewald Church held separate classes for boys and girls to instruct them in church history, church beliefs, and the Bible. Although Dietrich and Sabine attended separate classes, they did go to church together on Sundays and sometimes discussed the sermons. Dietrich devoted considerable time to independent Bible study and awoke early so that he would have time to read Scripture before breakfast each morning.

Soon after he was confirmed at age fourteen, he finally announced to the family his intention to become a theologian. At first his brothers and sisters didn't take him seriously, but the more they teased him about his choice, the more serious he became. Karl-Friedrich, who was studying natural science, and Klaus, who had begun his law studies, tried to convince their younger brother that the church was not worthy of his time and attention. According to family members, Dietrich exclaimed, "In that case I shall reform it!"[7] When Dietrich chose to take Hebrew as his optional subject in school and began attending church services with his mother, everyone realized that he was serious about the decision to study theology.

Looking back on Dietrich's decision, Eberhard Bethge suggests that there were several factors that influenced his choice. Even as a young child, Dietrich was fascinated with the idea of death and life eternal. Walter's death and his mother's grief renewed his own belief in eternal life and energized him to share that hope with others. He also felt a growing gulf between himself and his older brothers, all of whom had fought in the war and excelled in the sciences. Unlike them, he was drawn not to science but to spiritual matters, and his loneliness led him to God. At this time in his life, the study of theology did not involve church attendance or Bible reading, but took a more philosophical approach. His reading was wide and varied and included the early works of Hermann Hesse, various ancient Greek philosophers, and the German theologians Schleiermacher, Naumann, and his own great-grandfather Karl August von Hase. Having made his career decision, Dietrich seemed to his friends to be "radiant." As one friend said, "his high spirits knew no bounds."[8]

Although the family's life had resumed some of its former lightheartedness with family musical evenings and parties with friends, the Bonhoeffers were not immune to the problems troubling Germany. The economy remained in a disastrous condition. Millions of people found themselves in financial ruin. By 1923 the German mark which had been comparable to the U.S. dollar, was so devalued that one egg might cost 80 million marks, a glass of beer 150 million, and a pound of meat 3.2 billion marks. That the Bonhoeffers survived this period in relatively good condition was due to the fact that Karl Bonhoeffer, as a highly regarded psychiatrist treated patients who were able to pay him in foreign currency.

In the spring of 1923 Dietrich finished secondary school and headed to the university for the summer term. It was a Bonhoeffer family tradition to attend the university at Tübingen. Dietrich's father and brothers Karl-Friedrich and Klaus had chosen Tübingen, and his sister Christine was studying biology there when

Dietrich headed to university. The terrible inflation in Germany made university life difficult at first. Dietrich took the least expensive train to Tübingen from Berlin even though it took forty-eight hours. His father gave him one French franc to keep in his pocket for emergencies. In letters home during late October and early November 1923 Dietrich wrote, "every meal costs a billion. I had to pay 6 billion for bread. Margarine costs 20 billion. I also had to pay 35 billion for university dues. Laundry is enormously expensive. One starched shirt for a few days is 15 billion."[9] Just after he sent these letters, the inflation ended and the economy began to regain some of its stability. But, of course, Germany's biggest troubles lay ahead. Adolf Hitler and the Third Reich were on the horizon.

4

University Days

FOR THE NEXT FEW YEARS, Dietrich was able to devote himself to his studies and his first practical church work. However, during his university days Dietrich continued on a unwavering path toward resistance. At the time, of course, no one could imagine the horrors ahead, but the friends and experiences of university days certainly contributed to his unwavering commitment to stand strong against Hitler.

Among the most powerful influences in Dietrich's life was his grandmother, Julie Bonhoeffer. While he was at the university in Tübingen, Dietrich lived with her. Grandmother Bonhoeffer was a brilliant and fascinating woman who remained alert to political changes in Germany and the world. Years later, the family told with pride the story of the ninety-year-old grandmother's confrontation with Hitler's S.A. troops. When a boycott was placed on all Jewish businesses in April of 1933, she walked past the S.A. troopers and through the barricades to patronize a Jewish shop. "I buy my butter where I always buy it," she said to the S.A. troopers at the barricades before she entered the shop.[1] Long after he had left the university Dietrich continued to stay in touch with his grandmother through a lively exchange of letters. When she died in 1936, Dietrich spoke at her funeral. "For us, a world comes to an end with her, a world which we all somehow bear and want to bear within us. Right that does not compromise, free speech of a free person, the binding character of a word once given, clarity and plainness of speech, integrity and simplicity in private and public life—to this she was devoted with her whole life." Her last years were saddened, he continued, by "the great sorrow that she bore on account of the fate of the Jews in our nation."[2]

Dietrich's university experience was enriched by close friendships formed during his Tübingen days. Several of those friendships began within a fraternity called the "Hedgehog." One of his fraternity brothers later recalled that Dietrich seemed far older than seventeen. "I was no match for Dietrich Bonhoeffer's stormy temperament and self-confidence."[3] Dietrich reported that he liked these new friends and spent his time in study, playing piano, and debates with his fraternity brothers. Dietrich, who had set high standards for himself, selected lectures on the history of religion and philosophy. Fraternity brother Walter Dress, who was two years older than Dietrich, shared an interest in theology. Dietrich, always intense, enjoyed lively discussions and debates, and in Walter he found someone with whom he could spend hours talking about theology and church politics. They met again in classes in Berlin, and when Dietrich left Germany for work and study abroad, the two continued their debates through letters and postcards. Eventually Water Dress married Dietrich's younger sister Susi.

Membership in the Hedgehog provided Dietrich with an unusual military experience. Despite the provisions of the Versailles Treaty that prohibited Germany from developing a strong army, young men were secretly trained in military skills by the German army. The government had reason to fear that some of the German land, especially in the eastern regions, was in danger of being occupied by other countries. Students at Tübingen, as well as at other universities, were encouraged to participate in this illegal military training. Dietrich spent two weeks at Ulm training with other members of the Hedgehog. Although he was pleased that he withstood the physical training easily, he was happy to return to his comfortable bed and the good food at the university.

Shortly before his eighteenth birthday, Dietrich fell ice skating and remained unconscious for some time because of a concussion. His worried parents visited him in Tübingen and were relieved to find him recovering. When he asked his parents if he could spend a term studying in Rome, they agreed, and in the spring of 1924, Dietrich and his brother Klaus left on a three-month journey to Italy and North Africa.

Dietrich, who had a great gift for languages, taught himself Italian in preparation for the trip. He and Klaus traveled to Naples and Sicily and even spent ten days traveling through the deserts of North Africa. Rome, however, was his favorite city. He was thrilled by the great Catholic churches, especially St. Peter's and the church of Santa Maria Maggiore. Even more than the art and architecture of Rome, Dietrich was intrigued by the Catholic worshipers that he saw in the great cathedrals.

Dietrich and Klaus befriended a young priest in Bologna, who traveled with them to Rome and acted as a kind of religious tour guide. During Easter week, Dietrich attended a variety of masses and observed confession at both St. Peter's and Santa Maria Maggiore. He came to appreciate the seriousness with which the Catholics he observed participated in confession and worship. "Even the children," he noticed, "confess with a real ardor that is very moving to see."[4]

Dietrich remained in Rome a month longer than Klaus. During that time he continued to visit and study the historic sites and to attend lectures on religion and theology at one of the local colleges. When he left Rome in June, he wrote, "When I looked at St. Peter's for the last time there was a feeling of sadness in my heart, and I quickly got into the tram and went away."[5] His fascination with world churches, and particularly with the Catholic Church, had its roots in this visit to Rome. A few years later Dietrich served as a youth representative to a conference of the World Alliance of Churches and worked diligently to develop strong ties between peoples of different faiths. He eventually returned to Rome for a few days' visit in 1936 accompanied by Eberhard Bethge. As on the first visit, Dietrich was overwhelmed by the beauty of St. Peter's and was eager to share it with his friend.

In the fall of 1924, after one year at Tübingen and a summer of travel, the eighteen-year-old Dietrich returned to Berlin in time to register for classes at the University of Berlin, where he would study for the next three years. It was not unusual for a student in Germany at that time to transfer from school to school in order to take classes from particular professors or to broaden their studies into other areas, and several of Dietrich's fraternity brothers from the Hedgehog also transferred to Berlin. Dietrich plunged into theological studies; he not only read all the works of Martin Luther, but he memorized large portions of Luther's writings and was able to quote them from memory. He especially enjoyed his classes in systematic theology under Professor Reinhold Seeberg, who became his thesis advisor. As a student at the University of Berlin, Dietrich studied history, philosophy, and psychology in addition to his in-depth study of theology. He continued to read widely, and, during an attack of the flu in the winter of 1925, he read the plays of Ibsen and the theology of Karl Barth.

It was Dietrich's cousin and childhood friend Hans-Christoph von Hase, a physics student at the University of Göttingen, who first introduced Dietrich to the work of Swiss theologian Karl Barth. Barth was lecturing in Göttingen, and Hans-Christoph, captivated by Barth's new approach to theology, gave up his interest in atomic science and transferred to theology. Hans-Chrstoph sent Dietrich some of Barth's lecture notes, and Dietrich too was intrigued by the new ideas that Barth discussed.[6] Barth taught that God becomes known to individual people in particular times and places through preaching, through Bible study, and through Jesus Christ. Unlike most liberal theologians of the day, Barth focused on the spiritual aspects of God. Barth asked, How can the individual Christian better understand and approach God?

Dietrich, convinced that Barth had shifted theology into an exciting and fruitful area, argued at length with his professors during class discussions. His classmates expressed surprise that Dietrich was so bold as to challenge the faculty. One classmate later commented:

> I actually had the experience (and to me it was rather alarming and a tremendous novelty!) of seeing the young blond student contra-

dict the revered polyhistorian, His Excellency von Harnack, politely but on objective theological grounds. Harnack replied, but the student contradicted him again and again. I no longer know the topic of the discussion—Karl Barth was mentioned—but I still recall the secret enthusiasm that I felt for this free, critical and independent theological thought.[7]

Dietrich, still in his late teens, began to gather his own following of students eager to listen to his views on theology. They were attracted by his intelligence and enthusiasm for the subject, and by his willingness to help and support them in their studies. In many ways Dietrich was a loner, but others sought him out. Eberhard Bethge wrote that the Bonhoeffer family standards made it difficult for friends to find acceptance. However, once Dietrich did establish a friendship, it developed into a deep and abiding relationship more often than not characterized by intellectually stimulating discussion and a shared love of music.

One of the students Dietrich befriended was a young woman who was also studying theology. As their friendship developed, the two students, who enjoyed debating theological issues, spent so much time together that many friends assumed that they would marry. That was not to be. Although Dietrich stayed in touch with the young woman for many years, his mind turned increasingly to church politics and eventually to active political resistance to Hitler. He broke off the relationship with the woman in 1936. By that time she was a pastor herself.[8] Dietrich knew that the choice he was making to actively oppose Hitler would be dangerous, and he declined to continue the relationship in the midst of such tensions. It may have been, however, that this relationship was more intellectual than emotional, for in the midst of the most dangerous days of the Third Reich, Dietrich fell deeply in love and proposed marriage to another.

While he was in the midst of his studies, Dietrich had his first opportunity to act as a pastor. Such work was required of all theological candidates by church regulations. Dietrich was assigned the task of organizing a children's program at a German Evangelical church in the Grunewald district of Berlin. Every Sunday morning, with the children gathered around, Dietrich held them in rapt attention as he retold stories from the Bible. He followed the example set by his own mother when he was a child. Her stories were told with enthusiasm, and she often embellished the traditional Bible tales to add excitement and clarity. Dietrich enjoyed working with the children and knew that it was important work. He gave himself totally to the task, explaining to a friend that difficult theological concepts were worthless if they could not be explained to little children. Eventually Dietrich convinced his sister Susi to help with the classes, and sometimes Dietrich and Susi invited the children home for games or took them on outings.

As attendance soared, Dietrich worried that his own popularity was detracting from the real reason for attending the Sunday school. His vibrant personality and his tendency to attract admirers were a concern throughout his life. When he was in prison, it was not only fellow prisoners but also the prison guards who waited eagerly for a kind word from Prisoner Bonhoeffer. For a man who valued solitude, the church children, university students, and colleagues sometimes created a burdensome responsibility.

On Thursday nights Dietrich met with a group for older youths who had outgrown the children's program. These well-educated high school students discussed various religious, ethical, and political concepts as well as the cultural issues of the day. Dietrich usually began the evening by reading a short paper on a particular topic. Lively discussion followed. The youth group met socially and often went to an opera or a concert together. Dietrich prepared them for the experience by giving a talk about the performance. Afterwards they would discuss the event with the same kind of enthusiasm reserved today for movies or television programs.

Dietrich assumed that his youth group was capable of dealing with the most difficult aspects of religious faith, and they lived up to his expectations. Ahead of them lay the difficult moral decisions faced by all Germans during the Hitler years: to join the Nazis, to stand by and allow Nazi persecution, or to resist Hitler, help the Jews, and risk their own deaths. Unfortunately, most of the members of this group died on the battlefields or in the concentration camps of World War II.

During the mid-1920s Dietrich's family was changing in new and exciting ways. Only Dietrich and his youngest sister, Susi, lived at home. Karl-Friedrich, the oldest brother, became an assistant at the Kaiser Wilhelm Institute for Physics and Chemistry. Klaus ended his legal studies and become a practicing attorney, and Ursula married Rüdiger Schleicher. Dietrich's brothers and sisters and their wives and husbands gathered for family parties at the Bonhoeffer home, and Dietrich brought home friends from the university, as well. Many happy evenings were spent dancing and singing around the piano while Dietrich played. There were also serious discussions about the events of the day.

When Dietrich's twin sister, Sabine, became engaged to Gerhard Leibholz in 1924, her mother spoke with her at length about her choice. Although Gerhard, like his mother, was a Christian, his father was Jewish. Paula Bonhoeffer knew that Sabine's children would be considered Jewish and that life would not be easy for them in Germany. Although the Bonhoeffers liked Gerhard, they feared for Sabine.

Sabine understood their fears. In 1917 she had witnessed discrimination against a new classmate, a girl of English-Jewish descent. Sabine's friends had tried to exclude the girl from their activities, but Sabine had befriended her, and the Jewish child was eventually accepted. The next year two Jewish sisters were accepted at her school, and Sabine noticed even more resentment from classmates. She reported that "some little girls made so bold as to come to school with little silver swastikas round their necks."[9] The teacher forbade them from wearing the swastikas again, but the damage had been done.

Sabine, however, was not dissuaded by her parents' concerns or the growing anti-Semitism she witnessed at school or on the streets. Her feelings for Gerhard Leibholz were deep and abiding, and they were married in 1926. The next year, their daughter Marianne was born. Her baptism, held in the grandparents' home, was another festive celebration. Dietrich was delighted that

Sabine and Gerhard selected him as Marianne's godfather. Whenever Sabine brought little Marianne by, Dietrich eagerly took time from studying to play with the little girl and to visit with Sabine. Certainly Dietrich's love for his sister and his family played a role in his understanding of the anti-Semitism facing German citizens in the 1930s. He would be called on to help the Leibholz family flee Germany a decade later.

In 1927, when he was twenty-one years old, Dietrich wrote a dissertation, *The Communion of Saints*, to complete his theological studies. Dietrich declared that when the church is a true gathering of God's people into community, "standing under God's rule means living in community with God and with the church. . . ."[10] Dietrich's ideas about the church as community were years ahead of most scholars of his day and reflected his study of Barth and his own unique interpretation of Scripture. He wrote that "we shall see not only God but God's community too. We shall no longer merely believe in its love and faith, but see it. We shall know the will of God continually ruling over us and put it into practice in the kingdom of the community."[11] In this early work, Dietrich began to articulate an understanding of the role of the church in society, an idea that was strengthened by his exposure at Union Seminary in 1930 to American ideas of social justice and that eventually led him to speak out against the Nazis and in support of the Jews.

The night before Dietrich defended his thesis, he met Franz Hildebrandt, a fellow student at the university. While waiting for class to begin, they became involved in an intellectual argument over the importance of the Old Testament for Christian worship. Dietrich felt that it was of tremendous importance, while Hildebrandt argued the opposite. Dietrich eventually won Franz over to his point of view. The tone for their relationship had been set at that first meeting; intense intellectual debate characterized and strengthened a friendship that lasted a lifetime. When they were working on their university papers, they were able to test their ideas on each other before turning the results over to the faculty. Later, when preaching or involved in the church struggle, they continued to argue with one another as a means of testing and clarifying their ideas. Hildebrandt has written, "we continued arguing through twelve years of unbroken friendship, till the outbreak of the war made contact between England and Germany impossible . . . I did not know then how many years, how many dimensions, he was ahead of our whole generation." He added, that "having talked theology with him (and indeed not only theology) meant that one could never talk like that to anyone else again. . . ."[12]

Dietrich introduced Franz, who was three years his junior, into the Bonhoeffer family, where he was warmly welcomed. For Franz, an only child, the Bonhoeffer brothers and sisters became like his own family, and he spent many Sunday afternoons relaxing at their homes. His love of music (Franz also played the piano expertly), his keen intelligence, and Dietrich's high regard for him brought him acceptance into the family to such a degree that Dietrich's nieces and nephews eventually called him "Uncle Franz."

When Dietrich and Franz met in 1928, neither could have imagined that Franz would eventually be forced to leave Germany or face imprisonment because of his Jewish heritage. Hildebrandt, who had a Christian father and a Jewish mother, was raised a Christian, attended seminary, and became a Protestant pastor. However, under Hitler's anti-Semitic policies, Franz was labeled a Jew. When his Jewish background and his involvement in the church struggle threatened his safety in Germany, the Bonhoeffers aided and protected him and helped him escape to England.

5

Barcelona, Spain

1928

DIETRICH'S FAMILY HAD ALWAYS assumed that he was headed for an academic career as a theologian. Dietrich, however, had other ideas. Once his dissertation was completed, he received his first official assignment for the church; he would serve as assistant pastor to a German-speaking congregation in Barcelona, Spain. The Barcelona congregation consisted of German businessmen and their families. Dietrich began his assignment with enthusiasm. He visited church members in their homes in order to get to know them better and was disappointed to find that these Germans living abroad did not share his own intellectual curiosity. Rather, they avoided their Spanish neighbors and separated themselves from the Spanish culture in which they lived.

Dietrich learned Spanish and enjoyed life in Barcelona. He missed his family and the intellectual discussions among family and neighbors in Berlin, but his demanding schedule kept him occupied. He managed to find time to write many letters home and to record his thoughts in his diary. To his parents he wrote that he enjoyed the countryside around Barcelona and considered it among the most beautiful in Spain.

Dietrich plunged into his work, first by beginning a children's

Sunday school. Despite his enthusiasm, on the first Sunday only one small girl arrived. Dietrich visited those families with children and encouraged them to attend the Sunday classes. By the second Sunday, fifteen children attended, and on the third Sunday, thirty children came to the class. From then on thirty or more attended the class each Sunday and listened eagerly to Dietrich's Bible stories and lessons. Dietrich enjoyed being with the children, and the children loved him in return. When he planned the church's first ever nativity pageant, he was overwhelmed with their enthusiasm, and the program was nearly overrun with extra angels and shepherds.

As he had in Berlin, Dietrich also began a youth group for older boys. They gathered at his small apartment and discussed the Bible. Dietrich encouraged them to think about creation, sin, and the role of God in the universe. The boys enjoyed Dietrich and their classes so much that they wrote to him long after he had returned to Berlin.

Dietrich, who also preached at Sunday services, found that he had a knack for preaching. The congregation was enthusiastic about his sermons, and attendance at Sunday services increased dramatically. In fact, his preaching proved so popular that he was concerned that a rift might develop between the head pastor and himself. Dietrich was careful not to cause friction with the kindly Pastor Olbricht, who had welcomed him so graciously into the Barcelona congregation.

In his role as assistant pastor, Dietrich also worked at the German social welfare agency as part of his church duties. There he encountered people unlike any he had ever met. He wrote to his father:

> One has to deal with the strangest persons, with whom one would otherwise scarcely have exchanged a word, bums, vagabonds, criminals on the run, many foreign legionnaires, lion and other animal tamers who had run away from the Krone Circus on its Spanish tour, German dancers from the music halls here, German murderers on the run—all of whom tell one their life story in detail.[1]

He also met wealthy families who had suffered total financial ruin while in Spain. It was up to him to make the difficult decisions about whether or not to give aid to those who applied. "Kindness and friendliness," Dietrich wrote to his father, "is the best way of dealing with these people. . . ."[2]

While in Spain, Dietrich had the opportunity for more travel. When his brother Klaus visited, the two traveled to a number of Spanish cities: Toledo, Cordoba, Seville, Granada, and Algeciras. They even visited briefly in Morocco, in northwestern Africa. Dietrich's parents visited too, and he surprised them by taking them to a bullfight.

The entire Bonhoeffer family was shocked to learn that Dietrich, who had always been so tenderhearted, enjoyed going to the bullfights. As a child he had protested when a sand bomb thrown against the hen house upset the chickens. As a young man, he complained about the brutality of boxing matches. Now, it seemed as if he had no qualms about watching a man duel with a bull until it died. He wrote to his sister Sabine, "with every bull one becomes quicker at seeing beyond the element of sensationalism and cruelty." He went on to explain:

> . . . the swing from "Hosanna!" to "Crucify him!" has never been brought home to me so vividly as in the positively senseless roaring of the crowd when the torero makes a good pass, and the equally senseless screaming and whistling that follow immediately when some kind of bad luck befalls the same torero.[3]

Dietrich's gift for languages helped him to learn Spanish well enough that he could converse with the local people, and he was able to read Don Quixote in the original Spanish. He also joined a choral society and spent many hours playing piano at church social gatherings. He enjoyed going to the open-air market and purchased a number of treasured souvenirs. One, which remained controversial among his family and art experts, was a painting of a woman. It was signed, "Picasso." Whether or not it was actually painted by the famous Spanish artist was never resolved; the piece was destroyed when the Allied bombs hit Berlin in 1945.

While enjoying a year of political tranquillity in Spain, Dietrich paid little attention to the political atmosphere in Germany. He was so totally absorbed with practical church work and theological studies that he had no real interest in politics. He was always an avid newspaper reader, so while he knew what was going on, he simply focused his energies elsewhere. His brothers and brothers-in-law, on the other hand, had plunged into the midst of the swirl of political controversy in Germany, and they certainly kept Dietrich informed. As surely as the Weimar Republic was losing ground, the Nazis were becoming a political force in Germany. Economic instability returned, although without the extreme inflation of the early 1920s, and the constant challenge of groups on both the political right and the political left weakened the Weimar government and opened the door for the Nazis to grasp power. Adolf Hitler had been working to build up his NSDAP or Nazi Party, and he was bitterly disappointed by their poor showing in the German national elections held on May 20, 1928. Hitler spent the next two years reorganizing the party. He concentrated on building his strength in rural Germany.

For Dietrich, theological work overshadowed politics. Although the Barcelona congregation was eager for Dietrich to extend his stay in Spain, he decided to return to Berlin in February 1929 to resume his theological work. In order to become a university professor he would have to complete a second thesis. *Act and Being*, like his first thesis, focused on the church's role within society. In this thesis, which Eberhard Bethge describes as being "highly abstract," Dietrich wrote that the church must not withdraw from the day-to-day activities of people in the world if it is to remain true to the gospel.[4] All his writing and thinking led him to the conclusion that the church is a community that hears the preaching of the gospel and believes it. It responds through two acts: believing and loving. Dietrich wrote that the church must share in the secular problems of ordinary people and provide help and service to one another.

Dietrich's academic work was interrupted a number of times for happy family celebrations. His youngest sister, Susanne, married Dietrich's friend Walter Dress, who was working as a pastor in Berlin. Karl-Friedrich, his oldest brother, married Grete von Dohnanyi, and his brother Klaus married Emmi Delbrück. The family continued to gather for musical evenings, birthday celebrations, and holidays.

During 1929 Dietrich served as a voluntary assistant lecturer at the university. His duties were far from exciting: he handed out keys to students, supervised the library, and read student papers in order to detect plagiarism. On July 18, 1930, he qualified to give his first university lecture, but there was still no offer of a permanent position. Although he had completed his theological exams and a second thesis, Dietrich was simply not old enough for ordination because the church set the minimum age at twenty-five; Dietrich was only twenty-three.

When the opportunity to study in America became available, Dietrich at first dismissed it. He wasn't particularly interested in the United States and felt there was not much he could learn from American theologians. His dream at the time was to study in India with Gandhi. It may have been his Grandmother Bonhoeffer who first suggested India to Dietrich in a letter she wrote to him in Barcelona. "In your place I should try some time or other to get to know the contrasting world of the East, I am thinking of India, Buddha, and his world."[5] She even sent him some money toward such a trip, but the time was not right for a trip to India.

Eventually, with the offer of a prestigious Sloan Scholarship to study at Union Theological Seminary in New York City, Dietrich decided to accept the scholarship and go to the United States. Although he spoke English quite well, he devoted time during the Atlantic crossing to learning American expressions. Once he arrived in New York his natural curiosity led him to develop life-long friendships and to explore the United States with enthusiasm. His experiences in American churches and with American friends broadened his perspective. He still hoped that he could return to Berlin by way of India, but it proved too costly. He spent a relaxed summer holiday in Friedrichsbrunn before boarding a ship heading to the New World.

6

New York, New York

1930

D IETRICH CAME TO NEW YORK reluctantly, but he was
quick to embrace the opportunity. He was one of several
European students studying theology at Union Seminary
in 1930. Because he already held the equivalent of a doctorate
degree, Dietrich was ahead of most Union students. Paul
Lehmann, who became Dietrich's closest American friend, was
particularly impressed by Dietrich's theological knowledge, as
well as his unique personality. Lehmann and his wife, Marion,
often had Dietrich to their home, accompanied him to the movies,
and helped him learn to drive. Lehmann wrote that

> with people, he was as ready to listen as to speak, to identify as to
> analyze, participate as to investigate. One did not notice the soli-
> tude which prepared him for fellowship, the discipline which sus-
> tained his abandon, the quiet piety which nourished the acumen of
> his lively mind. One did not notice because a rare and gentle, some-
> thing rebuking but always compassionate humour, carried and
> concealed a faith in daily triumph over doubt, a human spirit to
> whom nothing human was alien.[1]

Dietrich was asked to speak to a number of student groups and
church groups. One Methodist church advertised his talk with the
following notice:

Dr. Deitrich Bonhoefier [*sic*], a professor of the University of Berlin, will speak. From the heart of Germany he will bring to us a message on "WAR." Did you ever wonder what the German people are thinking about war? This is an unusual opportunity to find out. Don't miss it![2]

He was surprised at the number of such requests he received. He wrote to his sister Sabine, "I am now continually and on the most varied occasions having to make speeches and deliver addresses . . . next week I am going to talk about Germany to more than 1,000 schoolchildren."[3] Whenever he spoke of his homeland, he emphasized Germany's desire for peace. During one such speech, he said, "As a Christian minister I think that just here is one of the greatest tasks for our church: to strengthen the work of peace in every country and in the whole world."[4] It soon became apparent, however, that the desire for peace was Dietrich's, not his country's.

Dietrich arrived in the United States on September 5, 1930, just a year after "Black Thursday," the stock market collapse that signaled the beginning of the Great Depression. Already at the end of 1929, factory closings, business failures, and bank collapses had put three million Americans out of work. On the streets of New York, he was exposed to political, economic, and social problems in the United States. He saw long lines of unemployed workers, cardboard shacks housing New York's homeless, and the dreary poverty of Harlem. One of his seminary classes, Church and Community, included visits to various social welfare agencies in New York. He wrote that he was impressed "to see how much personal self-sacrifice is achieved, with how much devotion, energy and sense of responsibility the work is done."[5]

The news from Germany was not reassuring. The effects of the Depression in the United States reverberated throughout the world. Dietrich stayed in touch with his family through letters. Their letters reported growing unemployment (affecting over four million workers by 1930), a Nazi gain of over one hundred seats in the recent election, and increasing anti-Jewish sentiment. At Berlin University, Jewish students were taunted with cries of "Death to the Jews," and Nazi flags began to appear in Christian churches. Klaus, Dietrich's older brother, wrote in a letter dated

March 11, 1930: "Fond glances are cast in the direction of Fascism. I am afraid that, if this radical wave captures the educated classes, it will be all up with this nation of poets and thinkers."[6]

While at Union, Dietrich discovered the vibrant, meaningful worship taking place in the churches of Harlem. Franklin Fisher and Dietrich Bonhoeffer were both minority students at Union: Fisher because he was a black student and Bonhoeffer because he was a foreign student. It was probably a combination of Dietrich's insatiable curiosity and his personal integrity that led Franklin Fisher to introduce Dietrich to the "Negro" community. At that time, the black and white communities in the United States were completely segregated. Dietrich was shocked by the racism he witnessed in New York. In fact, he and his oldest brother, Karl-Friedrich, spoke at length about the racial discrimination they both witnessed in America. Karl-Friedrich had turned down a teaching job at an American university to avoid exposing his own young children to a racially prejudiced society. Karl-Friedrich had written to Dietrich on January 24, 1931:

> I am delighted you have the opportunity of studying the Negro question so thoroughly. I had the impression when I was over there that it is really the problem, at any rate for people with a conscience and, when I was offered an appointment at Harvard, it was a very basic reason for my disinclination to go to America for good, because I did not want either to take on that legacy myself or to pass it on to my hypothetical children.[7]

Neither Dietrich nor Karl-Friedrich foresaw the anti-Semitic horrors ahead for their own country. At the time Karl-Friedrich suggested that the charges of anti-Semitism in Germany were "a joke" compared to the racial problems facing the United States.

Franklin Fisher had broken the color barrier by attending Union. Dietrich Bonhoeffer broke it again by participating in church life in Harlem. He not only worshiped and assisted in the Sunday schools; he was invited into homes where he had the opportunity to meet Harlem families and to learn what it meant to be black in a segregated America.

Dietrich's classmates at Union were surprised and amused by the zeal with which Dietrich pursued his interest in the Negro community. Paul Lehmann later wrote that Dietrich was received in Harlem as though he had never been an outsider at all. On one evening, when a number of students, including Franklin Fisher and Dietrich Bonhoeffer went to dinner at a New York restaurant, the restaurant refused service to Fisher because he was black. Dietrich objected loudly and left the restaurant in protest, amazing the other students, who accepted such prejudicial treatment as normal.

When Dietrich wrote of his time at Union, he said, "This personal contact with the negroes was for me one of the most pleasing and significant events of my American visit."[8] Like the Catholics he witnessed in Rome, the Baptists in Harlem worshiped with the emotional fervor of people who truly believed. While he could not bring such emotion to his own German people, he did tell his students about the spirited worship services and brought back to Germany several phonograph records of Negro spirituals and gospel songs. Six years later, when Dietrich was director of an illegal seminary in the German countryside, he and his students gathered around the phonograph to listen to songs like "Swing Low Sweet Chariot" and "Go Tell It on the Mountain." How different the songs must have sounded when sung by German seminarians struggling with English, but what happy memories they would have recalled for Dietrich Bonhoeffer. For Dietrich, who was by this time a prisoner in his native land, besieged by powerful but immoral leaders, the words "Let my people go" may have resonated as an all-too-familiar plea of his own.

Over Christmas 1930, Dietrich traveled to Cuba with Swiss student Erwin Sutz. Erwin Sutz and Dietrich shared not only a common language but also a consuming interest in the theology of Karl Barth. Erwin Sutz was also a pianist and shared Dietrich's love of music. Toscanini, in particular, gave them great joy. The two remained lifelong friends, and Sutz became an important contact outside Germany during Dietrich's missions for the Resistance.

Dietrich's other close friend during his Union days was Jean Lasserre, a student from France. Dietrich was surprised to find that Jean Lasserre was a pacifist, and as the two discussed and debated the Bible's mandates, Dietrich became convinced that Lasserre had chosen the right path. Bonhoeffer, Lasserre, and Sutz formed a natural alliance. All were Sloan scholars at Union Seminary, but it was provocative theological discussions on pacifism and Barthian theology that made for more than a friendship of convenience. Each one profoundly influenced the thinking of the others. It was Sutz, having studied with Karl Barth, who arranged a meeting between Dietrich and Barth, and it was Lasserre who led Dietrich to a greater understanding of pacifism.

Dietrich wanted to see more of the United States and Mexico. He invited Jean Lasserre to accompany him to Mexico, where they visited a friend of Lasserre's at Victoria Teachers' Training College. Dietrich was eager to go, but since neither he nor Lasserre drove, Dietrich first had to learn how to drive a car. The first time he took the test he failed, and according to Marion Lehmann, "He was crushed."[9] He tried two more times and failed each time. The Lehmanns suggested that he should bribe the tester, but Dietrich adamantly refused. Finally, he convinced Paul Lehmann to drive them as far as Chicago and then take the train home. By that time, Dietrich figured that he would be able to drive.

Dietrich and Jean Lasserre were invited to speak on the subject of peace. The students in Mexico were amazed that two men whose countries were always considered the greatest of enemies would join together to proclaim a message of peace. In a video-taped interview in the 1980s Jean Lasserre extolled Dietrich's speech and suggested that the speech "helped him to progress in the way of pacifism."[10] After a week's explorations in Mexico, Dietrich and Jean Lasserre returned to New York just in time for Dietrich to catch the boat home to Germany. They had traveled four thousand miles in the United States and another twelve hundred in Mexico. During their time together Lasserre had a profound effect on Dietrich and led him toward Christ's teachings on peace. According to Eberhard Bethge, Lasserre provided the initial impulse for Bonhoeffer's great book *The Cost of Discipleship*.

7

Pacifism
and Protests

1931–1932

D IETRICH RETURNED TO BERLIN in June of 1931 and moved
back into his parents' home. He made some arrangements
for the courses he would be teaching at Berlin University in
the fall and then left to spend three weeks attending a seminar
with Karl Barth in Bonn. Dietrich's Swiss friend Erwin Sutz, a student of Karl Barth, arranged for Dietrich to meet Barth, and on
July 23, 1931, Barth invited Dietrich to join him for dinner. Bonhoeffer's students later told of the first meeting between teacher
and student by recalling that during the seminar Dietrich quoted
Luther's statement "that the curses of the godless sometimes
sound better to God's ear than the hallelujahs of the pious."[1] Barth
was delighted and immediately took special note of this new student.

As for Dietrich, he finally had the opportunity to ask questions
of the man who had played such an important part in his own
thinking and writing. In a letter to Erwin Sutz on July 24, 1931,
Dietrich shared his impressions of Barth. "I have been impressed
even more by discussions with him than by his writings and his
lectures. For he is really all there. I have never seen anything like
it before and wouldn't have believed it possible."[2] Over the course
of the next several years, Dietrich and Karl Barth would continue

to meet and correspond, often disagreeing with one another, particularly in discussions on ethics. Dietrich continued to look to Barth for guidance in his thinking. In 1932 he wrote to Barth, "The brief hours we have been together during the year have succeeded in guiding my thoughts, which are always wanting to sink into 'godless' questions, and keeping them to the point."[3]

By the fall of 1931 Dietrich was engaged in numerous activities both for the university and for the church. In addition to teaching at the university, he worked as chaplain at the technical college and taught a confirmation class in a poor section of Berlin. His energies were directed not only to the local church, but he participated on the larger, world stage of church affairs through his involvement in a relatively new organization, the World Alliance of Churches. During the last week of August and the first weeks of September, he attended the annual conference of the World Alliance for Promoting International Friendship through the Churches, which was held in Cambridge, England. It was his conversations with Jean Lasserre in New York about pacifism that prompted Dietrich to learn more about the church's role as an agent of peace. The World Alliance was trying to help various church denominations move toward unity with one another at the congregational level. Dietrich was appointed a member of the Youth Delegation of the German Evangelical Church. A new ruling for this conference required that 50 percent of the delegates from each nation be considered youth delegates. According to the ruling, these younger members would have unrestricted participation in the events. The economic crisis in German had resulted in a severe lack of church funds for such travel. Dietrich willingly spent his own money to attend the conference and argued with German church officials about its importance. He believed that if the churches could get along together perhaps nations would also be able to establish peaceful relationships. Prompted by his increasingly strong pacifist leanings and by his dedication to the idea of the church as community of God, he entered the world scene with an incredible energy and a hopeful spirit. He wrote to his family from Cambridge that the World Alliance was doing urgently important work.

Although only twenty-five years old, Dietrich impressed the delegates at the conference with his ability as a speaker and as a leader. He was one of three young men appointed as honorary youth secretaries. His relative youth did not mean that he waited at the margins; rather he plunged into the center of this work that he felt was so vital. His job involved coordinating work for the World Alliance in Germany, central and northern Europe, Hungary, and Austria. Coordinating this effort, traveling, and planning conferences demanded much of his time after he returned to Germany.

Dietrich was clearly committed to the peace efforts promoted by the World Alliance. Germany, however, was not, and after only three years, the German section of the World Alliance was forced to dissolve. Dietrich's involvement in the World Alliance required him to travel to meetings throughout Europe and provided him with a number of important contacts that he later used while working with the military conspiracy to overthrow Hitler.

His work with the World Alliance assumed an added immediacy in light of the changes he was witnessing in Germany. The Nazis had surged ahead in the September 14, 1930, election. They received 6.4 million votes, making them the second largest party in Germany's Reichstag. Hitler staged rallies and spoke throughout the country in an effort to gain even more support. By the end of 1931 the Nazi Party had 800,000 members, and Hitler's S.S. troops numbered 15,000 and the S.A. totaled 225,000. The Nazis now controlled thirty-six German newspapers with 431,000 readers.

Six months after the Cambridge conference, Dietrich reported to those attending a youth committee meeting in London that the growing nationalism among theology professors in Germany was hindering his work. Few theology students shared Dietrich's pacifist worldview, and in fact, of the nearly one thousand students studying theology at Berlin University at the time, most supported Hitler on the basis of his avowed intention to build a strong Germany. At the end of 1930, some reports suggested that even in the seminaries, "more than half [the candidates for ordination] were followers of Hitler."[4] Like many Germans, these seminary students saw in Hitler's programs hope for Germany's troubled economy. They also believed Hitler's promises to leave the church alone, and they failed to recognize the growing sentiment against the Jews. When Hitler's attitude toward the church and the Jews became clear, many who had initially favored Hitler changed their minds—but it was too late. By then Hitler was firmly in control.

At the university Dietrich was an outsider, not accepted by the older faculty members because of his theology and his youth, and not accepted by some of the students because of his politics. Although Dietrich could choose what courses to teach at the university, his pay depended completely upon his ability to attract students to his lectures. Several students chose to attend Dietrich's lectures out of curiosity. After all, he was the youngest member of the faculty and not much older than the students.

The core of students who gathered around Dietrich, however, were anti-Nazi. Dietrich was interested in international relations and peace at a time when Germany was preparing for war. He publicly spoke against the Nazis at the very time when the Hitler government was preparing for the rearmament of Germany. Many of the students who gathered around Dietrich at Berlin University became his supporters during the church struggles. Many also attended his illegal seminary at Finkenwalde in 1936.

In addition to attending Dietrich's lectures, some of the students became part of a study group that met with him one evening a week in the room of Wolf-Dieter Zimmermann, his assistant. Dietrich's preferred teaching strategy was to ask questions and guide discussions. They gathered in Zimmermann's small room in groups of ten to fifteen to discuss theology. Dietrich enjoyed such informal evenings because they allowed a more natural exchange of ideas than did lecturing. The students learned to think clearly, to examine issues from all sides, and not to jump to premature conclusions. At the end of each evening, Dietrich treated them to drinks in a local beer cellar.

He also invited students to his parents' home and to the country. With his small stipend from the university he rented nine acres of land at Biesenthal and built a simple wooden hut. His students often gathered provisions and joined him for a weekend in the country. It was a very simple home, and the students had to clear away the dust, build a fire in the fireplace, and set up the few furnishings: some bedsteads, a few stools, and a table. Dietrich enjoyed catching up on his reading and walking through the countryside. In the midst of the hectic days of lectures and meetings, his country retreat provided peace and sunshine.

Dietrich's lectures and talks focused on issues of international cooperation, peace, and the role of the church in the world. He delivered a talk in the fall of 1932 sponsored by the German Student Christian Movement. He emphasized that God is the God of all peoples and nations, not just of Germany. At a time when Germany was becoming increasingly militant, Dietrich Bonhoeffer said, "every form of war service, unless it be Good Samaritan service, and every preparation for war, is forbidden for the Christian."[5]

One series of lectures at Berlin University was so popular that his students convinced Dietrich to publish it. The lectures, published under the title *Creation and Fall* analyzed the first three chapters of Genesis. Dietrich did not usually teach about the Old Testament, and although the scholars in this field were not enthusiastic about his work, his students found his ideas provocative.

Dietrich's students and friends were impressed not only by his knowledge but also by his personal faith. As a child he had practiced religion in a childlike way—singing favorite hymns and saying simple prayers. As a university student, and even as a pastor in Barcelona, he had studied and spoken about religion as an academic subject. It was not until his return from America at the age of twenty-five that Dietrich began to live life fully committed to the teachings of Christ. He attended church services regularly, meditated daily on Bible passages, and included prayer and confession as a daily part of his life. He encouraged pacifism among his students and frequently cited the Sermon on the Mount as a blueprint for Christian action. He considered the Bible to be God's message of love to his people. In a letter to a friend in 1936, he recalled the earlier period of his life with remorse and noted with joy the change in his personal faith that occurred in 1931 32. He wrote in a letter to a friend:

> I know that at that time I turned the doctrine of Jesus Christ into something of personal advantage to myself. . . . I pray to God that

will never happen again. Also I had never prayed, or prayed only very little. For all my loneliness, I was quite pleased with myself. Then the Bible, and in particular the Sermon on the Mount, freed me from that. Since then everything has changed. I have felt this plainly, and so have other people about me. It was a great liberation. It became clear to me that the life of a servant of Jesus Christ must belong to the church, and step by step it became clearer to me how far that must go.[6]

On November 15, 1931, Dietrich was ordained in St. Matthew's Church in Berlin as a minister of the German Evangelical Church. His ordination was a quiet ceremony, and Dietrich seemed to attach little importance to it. He was asked to serve as student chaplain at the Technical University in Charlottenburg as part of an obligation for voluntary service to the church. In October he had written a letter to his friend Erwin Sutz, expressing his wish

that I could go somewhere into the country to get out of the way of everything that is wanted and expected of me. It is not that I am afraid of disappointing—at least I hope not that primarily—but that sometimes I simply cannot see how I am going to get things right. And the cheap consolation that one is doing one's best, and that there are people who would do it still worse, is unfortunately not always sufficient.[7]

Dietrich held the position of student chaplain for two years, and in fact it was not a success. He had difficulty getting recognition among the students. Notices he posted were torn down. The students, who were technicians and scientists, had little interest in theology and did not attend the services and lectures that Dietrich offered. When he left the job in 1933, no one was appointed to succeed him.

As Dietrich so eloquently stated in his letter to Sutz, much was expected of him during this time. He frequently served as guest preacher in various Berlin churches. And, while he loved preaching and found it challenging, sermon writing was also a demanding task. As he told his friend Franz Hildebrandt, "Every sermon must be an event."[8] Dietrich's preaching focused on Christ as peacemaker. His sermons were always biblically based, but he did not hesitate to discuss the political situation in Germany in light of God's commands.

Dietrich's previous work with children's services and youth ministry made him the ideal candidate to teach a confirmation class in the Zion parish in Wedding, a section of Berlin where unemployment and poverty were the rule, not the exception. The boys were extremely difficult and had a history of disruptive behavior. When Dietrich first entered the boys' classroom, there was total pandemonium. The church's pastor tried to gain order and failed. Dietrich, however, simply leaned quietly against the wall. Minutes passed, but the teacher said nothing. The boys were puzzled that he failed to yell at them or try in any way to calm them. They gradually became quieter. When Dietrich began speaking softly only the boys in the first few seats could hear him.

Suddenly the room was silent. Dietrich remarked that they had put on quite a show. Then he began telling them about his experiences in Harlem. He stopped after a short time and promised more stories the next time they met. From then on he never had a problem. He told the boys Bible stories, and as they began to understand more, he discussed the difficult topics of confirmation with them. In writing to his Swiss friend Erwin Sutz about the class he said,

> At the beginning the young lads behaved crazily, so that for the first time I had real problems of discipline. . . . Now there is absolute quiet, the young men see to that themselves, so I need no longer fear the fate of my predecessor, whom they quite literally worried to death.[9]

Dietrich found the work rewarding, and he could see that the boys were benefiting, so he eagerly gave them his time and his resources. On Christmas he gave each of the boys a gift. When one became ill, Dietrich took the time to visit him in the hospital. He taught the boys chess and English. He rented an apartment nearby and invited the boys to visit anytime and left word with the landlady that the boys could use the apartment even when he was not home. Such trust was a unique experience for these boys. They had never experienced the sunshine and fresh air of the German countryside until Dietrich took them on two-week outings to his parents' summer home in Friedrichsbrunn. After he rented the land in Biesenthal, he invited the boys from Wedding to spend time there whenever they liked. When the time of their confirmation arrived, he purchased bolts of cloth to be used for their confirmation suits.

On March 13, 1932, Dietrich preached at the confirmation service for his Wedding boys. In the two years he had spent with them he had tried to prepare them to live as Christians in the world. But the world was changing. On the very day that they were confirmed, national elections were held and Hitler was one of the candidates for the presidency. Many years after the war, Richard Rother, one of the boys in the confirmation class recalled those days with the words, "Never before or after has Zion Church had such a strong congregation as when this gifted man was its pastor."[10]

In addition to working with the confirmation class in Wedding, Dietrich helped to establish a youth club in Charlottenburg which opened in the fall of 1932. These older youths were unemployed. Some were troublemakers; others were active communists. The youth club was not connected with a particular church. A friend of Dietrich's sister Susi, Anneliese Schnurmann, contributed much of the money for the project. Once Hitler was in power, however, Anneliese Schnurmann, who was Jewish, decided to leave Germany. The communist members of the club were attacked in the streets, and the club itself was searched and eventually closed down by Hitler's police force, the Gestapo. Dietrich helped a few young communist club members to escape from Berlin. He hid them in his hut in Biesenthal until they could safely return to Berlin undetected by the Nazi police. Dietrich had no choice but to close the club. Dietrich realized that its closing marked one more loss of freedom caused by the Nazis' rise to power.

For many people, though, the rise of the Nazis seemed like good news. At last, many people said, we will have some order. Hitler promised work, which meant food and shelter for hungry families. He even promised the people's car, the Volkswagen, for all workers. For the many Germans who were hungry and unemployed, the sight of prosperous Jewish shops and the signs of wealthy Jewish doctors, lawyers, and professors caused resentment. They avoided noticing that there were also Jews living in

poverty, just as there were wealthy Christians who seemed unaf-
fected by economic misfortune. Hitler played on these growing
anti-Jewish sentiments. People who met or heard Hitler speak in
the 1930s were mesmerized by him. An American reporter,
William Shirer, who observed a Nuremberg party rally, wrote:

> About ten o'clock tonight I got caught in a mob of ten thousand
> hysterics who jammed the moat in front of Hitler's hotel, shouting:
> "We want our Führer." I was a little shocked at the faces, especially
> those of the women when Hitler finally appeared on the balcony
> for a moment. . . . They looked up at him as if he were a Messiah,
> their faces transformed into something positively inhuman.[11]

Military, political, and religious leaders inside Germany, as well
as presidents and kings outside of Germany, all fell under the
sway of Hitler's promises. Many Christian pastors saw in Hitler a
return to strong moral principles. According to German church
figures, in 1932, 215,908 people left the church and only 49,700
joined. In 1933, the Nazis actually encouraged church attendance
and the churches saw an abrupt reversal in their membership sta-
tistics. As a result 323,618 joined the church and only 56,849 left.

Hitler promised to turn the unruly youth of Germany into a dis-
ciplined citizenship. Once he established the Hitler Youth, Hitler
claimed that young people would learn how to think and act German. Of course, Hitler's goal was to create not a free people but an
army who would serve him without question.

Hitler's oratory mesmerized, and he did not hesitate to call on
religious fervor. In the early days, he compared himself to Christ.
"Just like Christ, I have a duty to my own people."[12] Nazi leaders
encouraged people, especially children, to accept this comparison.
A song popular in the *Jungvolk* a German boys' organization
included the words

> Adolf Hitler is our Saviour, our hero
> He is the noblest being in the whole wide world.
> For Hitler we live,
> For Hitler we die.
> Our Hitler is our Lord
> Who rules a brave new world.[13]

Dietrich distrusted Hitler's rhetoric from the beginning. He was one of the first to speak out against Hitler and Nazism and to see that Hitler's way would ultimately destroy the country and the people he loved. Dietrich had been nurtured in a strong intellectual family whose natural inclination to think clearly and to listen closely made them suspicious of Hitler's claims. The Bonhoeffers knew that there were no easy solutions to the political, economic, and social problems facing Germany; they recognized the dangers that Nazism posed for Germany and the world, and they gave each other the strength to act on their beliefs. Franz Hildebrandt, a frequent visitor to the Bonhoeffer home during the years leading up to Hitler's takeover, noticed that "in the midst of the general capitulation on the part of the German intelligentsia the Bonhoeffer family, his parents, brothers, sisters and the old grandmother, stood with unclouded vision and unshaken will; their house in Berlin-Grunewald, soon my second home by adoption and grace, was an oasis of freedom, fresh air and good humour."[14] In the 1930s, there was also an air of innocence. The Bonhoeffers could not imagine and did not predict where Hitler's ideas would ultimately lead.

8

Speaking Out

1933

O N JANUARY 30, 1933, Hitler was appointed chancellor. Two days later Dietrich gave a radio broadcast critical of the Führer. Dietrich's friend Wolf-Dieter Zimmermann, who worked for the radio station, had arranged for Dietrich to give the religious address directed to young people. In the speech entitled "The Younger Generation's Altered View of the Concept of Führer," Dietrich presented a clear warning to his listeners against following Hitler when he said, "leaders or offices which set themselves up as gods mock God."[1]

Suddenly, without explanation, the microphone was turned off. Dietrich finished his speech, but the radio transmission was lost. At that moment Dietrich and his family realized that the Nazis were already censoring radio broadcasts. Dietrich, who was deeply troubled by this attempt to muzzle him, had the speech duplicated and sent copies to family members and friends. In a lecture on the same theme delivered in March to students at the German High School for Politics, Dietrich said that a leader who allows his followers to make him into an idol will become a "misleader, and he will be acting in a criminal way not only toward those he leads, but also towards himself."[2]

On February 2, 1933, the government enacted the first Emergency Ordinance, which prohibited open-air meetings or parades. This effectively stopped all demonstrations against Hitler and his government. Anyone distributing leaflets, posters, or newspapers contrary to the Nazi government was subject to imprisonment. Anyone who knew of such activities and did not report them could be arrested.

Dietrich continued to preach in Berlin churches on Sundays and to teach at the university. He spoke boldly in his sermons, always staying close to a Bible text, but providing anyone who wanted to listen with warnings that they could apply to the political situation in Germany. In a February sermon he said, "Do not desire to be strong, powerful, glorious and respected, but let God alone be your strength, your fame and your honor."[3]

On February 27, 1933, the Reichstag, the main government building, was burned to the ground by a young communist protester. The fire gave Hitler the excuse he was looking for to tighten his grip on the German people. The government enacted the Reichstag Fire Edict, which abolished the basic rights of personal freedom. This edict declared that people could be arrested and detained by the government without reason. On March 23, 1933, the government enacted the Enabling Law, which abolished the basic principles of democracy and gave Hitler's government the power to enact laws without the consent of the Reichstag, to abandon the constitution at will, and to make treaties with foreign governments. When Hitler began to use these broad powers, he trampled such individual democratic rights as freedom of speech; freedom from unlawful search, seizure, and arrest; and freedom to own property. Censorship became the rule, and few dared speak out against the Nazis for fear of arrest. Homes were searched without warrants, property seized, and telephones tapped. The S.A. and the S.S., the police arms of Hitler's government, went to work immediately to enforce the new laws. By October 1933 between five and six hundred persons had been killed and over twenty-six thousand arrested as a direct result of these laws. The German people began to adjust to the Nazi demands, and that gradual acceptance, combined with brutal police power, ultimately guaranteed Adolf Hitler total control over the thoughts and actions of the German people.

At a time when almost no one could be trusted, the Bonhoeffer family remained intensely devoted to one another. They often gathered at Karl and Paula Bonhoeffer's home in Berlin to discuss the political situation. They covered the telephone with a pillow in case the Nazis were listening through a wiretap. They spoke softly, checked the doors for eavesdroppers, and developed a code language to further protect these political discussions. While they were not under direct police surveillance, they worried that the household help might overhear and report family conversations. The adults warned the young nieces and nephews that overheard conversations must not be mentioned outside of the house. Two of those children, Renate and Dorothee Schleicher remember being sent outside to make sure that no one was listening at the windows. No one realized at the time that the family would play a significant role in the opposition, but even at this early stage, the children were aware that their parents and grandparents discussed secrets and that they should not repeat certain things outside of the home.[4]

When Hitler introduced the Aryan Clause, which banned all those of Jewish ancestry from civil service jobs, he expected the clergy, who were considered state employees, to sign the pledge without protest. Under this edict, Dietrich's friend, Franz Hildebrandt, whose mother was Jewish, would no longer be able to serve as a Christian minister. Dietrich was stunned. He had hoped to serve in a parish with Hildebrandt. In an act reminiscent of his refusal to eat in a New York restaurant that would not serve Franklin Fisher, Dietrich declared that if his friend Franz Hildebrandt could not serve a German parish, then neither would he.

The boycott of Jewish shops organized by anti-Jewish demonstrators on April 1, 1933, further heightened his concern. Members of the S.A. stood guard at Jewish shops to prevent shoppers from entering. It was during this boycott that Dietrich's grandmother made her stand, an event that became something of a family legend, varying slightly depending on who was telling the tale.

Seven days later Jews were banned from the civil service. Dietrich worried about his sister Sabine's family. Her husband, Gerhard Leibholz, worked for the state as a professor. Under the Aryan laws, he would be dismissed from his job at the university. Fearing for his family's safety, Gerhard purchased a car for a possible escape from Germany.

In early April, Dietrich's friend from his Union Seminary days, Paul Lehmann visited him in Berlin. Lehmann had traveled from the United States to Bonn to hear Karl Barth speak and stopped for a few days' visit with his friend. He noted that as he visited with Dietrich and his brother Klaus in the Bonhoeffer home, Klaus would check from time to time to make sure no one was listening outside the door. They certainly spoke of issues and events that could place them in a dangerous position. Dietrich and Paul Lehmann talked about Hitler and predicted that he would not be in power for long. Dietrich expressed concern over the new Enabling Laws. After much discussion, the two men drafted a letter to Rabbi Stephen Wise in New York that reported the enactment of anti-Jewish laws in Germany and anticipated their effect. Even reporting this news was an act in violation of the new High Treason laws, but Dietrich willingly accepted the personal danger in order to get word to the Americans. Dietrich, who had heard Rabbi Wise preach in New York, was aware of the rabbi's friendship with President Roosevelt and hoped that Rabbi Wise would inform the President. A letter from Roosevelt to the rabbi clearly indicates that Dietrich's message was sent on to the President of the United States. It was quite probably the first word from Germany about the dangers facing German Jews.[5]

At the same time that Dietrich and Paul Lehmann were sending word to Roosevelt, a growing movement within the German Evangelical Church lent support to the Nazi policies. A group of pastors and church members who called themselves German Christians saw in Hitler's rise to power increased influence for the German church. They actively promoted a nationalistic church, and on April 3 4, 1933, they held the Reich Conference of German Christians in Berlin. In a June 1933 speech, one German Christian leader declared:

If anyone can lay claim to God's help, then it is Hitler, for without
God's benevolent fatherly hand, without his blessing, the nation
would not be where it stands today. It is an unbelievable miracle
that God has bestowed on our people.[6]

The beliefs that the German Christian Faith Movement promoted were not focused on the Bible, the traditional confessions
of the Christian faith, or the teachings of Jesus Christ. Instead, the
German Christians claimed that God worked through nature and
history. They labeled their teachings "positive Christianity" and
twisted the Christian faith to support Hitler's anti-Jewish actions.
The German Christians developed the image of a masculine
church which encouraged men to join police and military groups,
women to marry and have many Aryan children, and the children
to pay homage to Germany and Germanism rather than to Christianity. Since the German Christians claimed that God worked
through nature and race, only those deemed racially pure could
be German Christians. Anyone of mixed Christian-Jewish heritage was unwelcome. In a brochure originally written in 1935,
Cajus Fabricius, a theology professor from Breslau who was influential in the German Christian movement, put into words the
clear mandate of this group, "We oppose the mixture of our race
with that of the Jews."[7]

The German Christians were not a separate religious denomi-
nation. Rather they formed a movement within the German Evangelical Church. Its origins are mixed. In the late 1920s two young
pastors, both members of the Nazi Party preached religious
renewal based on German nationalism. They called themselves
German Christians. In the summer of 1932 another group of politicians and church people met in Berlin to look at ways to connect
the church and its resources with the National Socialist movement. Some accounts indicate that it was Hitler himself who suggested the name German Christians for this group, and eventually
the two groups with the same name began to work together. Other
groups promoting both religious values and German nationalism
merged with the German Christians giving them a broad base of
supporters. The German Christians remained a part of the German Evangelical Church and tried to convert all members of the

church to their particular pro-Nazi beliefs and, eventually, to remove all pastors who did not accept those beliefs. At first the movement was small, but as Hitler gained power, the German Christian Faith Movement gained momentum too. Some pastors actually wore the swastika on their clerical robes.[8]

Initially Hitler had promised to leave the churches alone. On June 28, 1933, Hitler responded to a question about the churches by saying, "I have nothing to do with church matters and don't want anything to do with them. I am gradually getting fed up with them."[9] The German Christians, however, craved Hitler's attention and coveted a close relationship with the Führer. Hitler, recognizing the growing strength of the German Christian movement, began to seek the support of these outspoken church leaders for his social and political plans. Nazi S.A. men, Hitler's storm troopers, went to church in their brown shirts and often started brawls and pro-Hitler demonstrations both inside and outside of the church doors.

Not all congregations or clergy supported the German Christians. By law all ministers of the German Evangelical Church were considered civil servants and, as such, were obligated to support the government. Of the eighteen thousand Protestant pastors in Germany in the mid-1930s, about a third became strong supporters of the German Christian movement. Another third stood by, watching, waiting, and hoping that they could avoid political entanglements. These pastors felt that their job was to preach and teach the Bible, not to become involved in the affairs of the world. Another third sought to return the church to its traditional biblical values and realized that to do so, they must speak out against the teachings of the German Christians. As time went on, the balance shifted until the voice of the true church was a distant whisper.

Hitler's support of the German Christians caused an initial increase in church membership, but Hitler's support was short-lived, and the church began to lose its power. Hitler eventually demanded that all boys and girls belong to the Hitler Youth, and since Hitler Youth meetings were held on Sunday mornings, church participation became impossible. Children and young people, as well as their parents, paid dearly for choosing church

Dietrich and his twin sister, Sabine, at age eight.

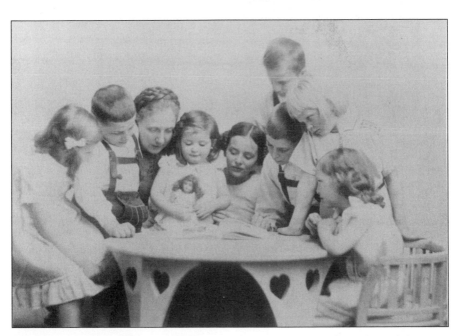

Paula Bonhoeffer and her eight children (Dietrich is second from the right).

Dietrich at age eleven.

Dietrich at about age sixteen.

On vacation in Rome at age eighteen.

Christmas in Barcelona, 1938.

At the Fanö Conference with Jean Lasserre, 1934.

Dietrich at the first seminary site in Zingst, 1935.

Eberhard Bethge and Dietrich at Gross-Schlönwitz in 1938.

Christmas 1940 in Ettal with the von Dohnanyi children and
Eberhard Bethge (playing flute).

Karl Bonhoeffer's seventy-fifth birthday party, March 31, 1943, five days before Dietrich's arrest (Dietrich is at far left edge of photo).

One of the last pictures of Dietrich, taken in the summer of 1944 at Tegel Prison.

over state. They might lose opportunities for further schooling, be denied jobs, or be sent to government work camps. Nevertheless, some courageous young people and their parents chose to remain active in traditional church activities.

Dietrich Bonhoeffer watched all that was happening in the church with great concern. He belonged to a small group of ministers who met for Bible study and discussion. It was for this group that he originally wrote a paper called "The Church and the Jewish Question." The paper, later published in a German theological journal, was the first public defense of the Jews in the face of the repressive laws being enacted in Germany. In his thesis he suggested three possible actions for the church. First, he suggested that the church can require the state to answer for its behavior—are its actions legitimate? Second, the church can assist any victims of state action. "The church," he wrote, "has an unconditional obligation to the victims of any ordering of society, even if they do not belong to the Christian community." Finally, he suggested a third possibility, "not just to bandage the victims under the wheel, but to jam a spoke in the wheel itself."[10] Kenneth C. Barnes suggests in his article "Dietrich Bonhoeffer and Hitler's Persecution of the Jews" that

> in this essay lies the blueprint for Bonhoeffer's response to the persecution of the Jews for the rest of his short life. The essay outlined three positions that he would take in successive phases of his career, which I will term (1) a call to qualified obedience, which characterizes his stance in 1933 1934; (2) a call to suffering, which described his views from 1935 to 1939 and is most visible in his work *The Cost of Discipleship;* and (3) a call to resistance, which eventually brought him to prison and his death in 1945.[11]

It is certainly in the second and third points that Dietrich moved beyond a weak response reflecting the anti-Semitism of his age and into new uncharted territory. However, even his suggestion that the church should question the state was too much for his 1933 audience. When Dietrich delivered his paper, some pastors got so upset that they left the room. Dietrich's suggestion that the church should assist those being persecuted by the state or his more radical call for political action against the state were too drastic for most church leaders of the time to even consider. They accepted and felt comfortable with the idea that there are two kingdoms, and a person—or a church—should "give therefore to the emperor the things that are the emperor's, and to God the things that are God's" (Matthew 22:21). Hitler had promised to leave the church alone, and the majority of church leaders apparently believed that the church should separate itself from the turmoil of the world. For them the church had become a quiet place of sanctuary.

The reaction to this paper foreshadowed the issues of the church struggle. Much of the Dietrich's paper dealt with the question of baptized Jews, and it is this group that Dietrich defends most strongly, declaring that "the forced expulsion of Gentile-Christian Jews from Gentile-Christian congregations of German race is in no case permissible. . . ."[12] The German Evangelical Church pastors who were not sympathetic to the German Christians agreed with Dietrich concerning the need to recognize and include within the church those Jews who had converted to Christianity. The argument was essentially theological. To remove from the Christian church anyone who had converted by baptism was to invalidate the sacrament of baptism and therefore the Bible, the teachings of Christ, and the confessions of faith on which the church was formed. To rely on race or ethnic origin to determine whether or not a person could become a Christian was to accept the German Christian call for exclusion of all non-Aryans from the church. Although there were actually not many Jewish-Christians in Germany, two people important to Dietrich fell into this category. They were Dietrich's friend Franz Hildebrandt and his sister Sabine's husband, Gerhard Leibholz.

Far more important and inflammatory were Dietrich's suggestions that it was the church's responsibility to assist the Jews and, if necessary, to take action against the state. Whenever Dietrich spoke openly in sermons or lectures or wrote articles that disagreed with Hitler's government, he knowingly placed himself in danger, but his conscience would not allow him to be quiet. One of his most often quoted Bible passages—"Speak out for those who cannot speak" (Proverbs 31:8)—drew attention to the plight of the voiceless Jews. Among his church colleagues, Dietrich seemed alone in his understanding that anti-Semitism would ultimately destroy a people and a nation. Dietrich believed that the church could not support Hitler and remain Christ's church. He believed that the church must participate in the activities of the world and support all who suffer injustice and discrimination.

Many of his colleagues urged Dietrich to wait and see what happened. But how could he stand idly by when he began to see where Hitler's intentions would lead? He joined a group of pastors who called themselves Young Reformers. The group was not radical enough to please Dietrich, but at least they shared some of his concerns and had spoken out strongly in favor of allowing Christians of Jewish descent to remain in the church.

On April 11, 1933, Gerhard Leibholz's father died. Sabine and Gerhard asked Dietrich to conduct the funeral service. Although the elder Leibholz was Jewish, he did not attend synagogue. He had liked and appreciated the young Christian pastor, and Gerhard felt that it would be appropriate for Dietrich to preside at the funeral, but Dietrich said no. His church superintendent and others advised him against conducting a service for a Jew at such a politically volatile time. It was a decision that Dietrich always regretted, and one that probably made his commitment to aid the Jews even stronger. He later wrote to Sabine and Gerhard:

> Now it is a matter of constant remorse to me that at that time I did not quite simply accede to your request. Frankly, I no longer understand myself in the least. How could I have been so horribly timid at that time? Certainly you have not really understood this, either, and have not said anything to me about it. But it haunts me now as something quite dreadful, the more so because it is something that now can never be made good. Today, therefore, I must simply beg you to forgive me for my weakness at the time. Today I know for sure that I should have acted otherwise.[13]

In the midst of the church upheaval, Dietrich continued lecturing at the university. His lectures revealed his strong feelings about the role of the church in society, and he gathered around him a group of students who shared his vision. They would later become some of the strongest supporters of the Confessing

Church, the unofficial organization of pastors who opposed the German Christian Faith Movement and Hitler's policies. Dietrich found time in the midst of the church struggle to have lively conversations with his students and to join his family in musical evenings. His mother was particularly interested in the church struggles, and Dietrich made a point of keeping her well informed. During later years when Dietrich was director of a seminary many miles from Berlin, he called her almost daily, an act of love that impressed his students. One wrote, "What an example Bonhoeffer set for us in his close attachment to his mother!"[14]

In sermons and meetings, Dietrich continued to suggest that the church must stand strong against wrongdoing by the state. He proclaimed that the church needed a new declaration of faith, a suggestion that was later seconded by Karl Barth. Despite his dissatisfaction with the German Evangelical Church, Dietrich tried to work within existing church structures. By 1933 the church was divided into three groups: the German Christians, who were fully supportive of the Nazi government; the Young Reformers, who opposed Hitler's Aryan Clause; and those who remained neutral or uncommitted to either side. In the important election of church officials scheduled for July 1933 the Young Reformers hoped to prevent the German Christians from taking control of the churches.

9

The Church Elections

1933–1934

THE BATTLE FOR CONTROL of the churches escalated rapidly during the church elections of April 1933. Dietrich Bonhoeffer, Martin Niemöller, the pastor St. Anne's in the Dahlem section of Berlin, and the Young Reformers worked feverishly to support their candidate, Bishop Friedrich von Bodelschwingh, director of a community for the disabled located at Bethel in Westphalia. Dietrich gave speeches and lectures in favor of Bodelschwingh and the ideals of the traditional German Evangelical Church, which Bodelschwingh represented. Dietrich spoke about the importance of the church confessions and of maintaining a unified church true to the teachings of Jesus Christ.

The German Christians, however, attacked Bodelschwingh's character. Their candidate for Reich Bishop, Ludwig Müller, had close ties to Hitler and had appeared at Hitler's side during public events. Because Bodelschwingh was highly esteemed by the German people in general, the German Christians' attacks on his character did not result in Bodelschwingh's defeat, but may have resulted in a smaller victory than the Young Reformers had predicted. Dietrich and Franz Hildebrandt, who had been working tirelessly for the victory, were pleased but disappointed that there had not been more support for Bodelschwingh, who they felt represented the true Christian church in Germany.

On the Sunday after the election, Dietrich was scheduled to preach at Berlin's Kaiser Wilhelm Memorial Church and Franz Hildebrandt would preach before another congregation. Each of them included comments about the church elections in their sermons. They suggested that those who had not supported Bodelschwingh should be ashamed of their actions. Franz's remarks were more direct; Dietrich, as was his custom, couched his comments in the context of the day's Bible lesson.

Although the election of Bodelschwingh seemed to signal a return to sensibility within the church, the victory was short-lived. Bodelschwingh had barely moved to Berlin before Müller and the German Christians increased their attacks on the new Reich Bishop in an effort to regain power. The universities, largely controlled by the Nazis, rallied support against Bodelschwingh. The German Christians organized a major campaign involving student groups, called German Christian Students' Fighting Leagues. On June 19, 1933, they held a large meeting at Berlin University attacking Bodelschwingh.

Dietrich and many of his university students attended. The students spoke out against the German Christian platform. Dietrich himself remained silent, waiting for the moment when he and several others had planned a surprise walkout if the German Christians called for a new election of Ludwig Müller. When a resolution was presented that supported Müller's candidacy for bishop, 90 percent of those present left the auditorium. This strong reaction against the German Christians gave the Young Reformers hope.

Four days later, on June 22, when the university chaplains held their own meeting to counter the German Christian attacks, Dietrich was one of the speakers. Although he spoke of a church struggle, he didn't realize at the time that the church was already irreparably divided and that it would remain so for the duration of Hitler's reign. Only two days later, on June 24, Bodelschwingh resigned, and on June 28, Ludwig Müller, backed by the Nazis,

ordered the S.A. to occupy the church offices in Berlin. In many
churches a message read from the pulpit declared:

> All those who are concerned for the safe structure of our church in
> the great revolution of these times, must . . . feel deeply thankful
> that the state should have assumed, in addition to all its other tasks,
> the great load and burden of reorganizing the church.[1]

Another church election was scheduled for July 1933. It was certainly rigged, and it was obvious that the German Christians
would win. Nevertheless, Dietrich, Franz Hildebrandt, Gerhard
Jacobi, a pastor who later became the president of the Confessing
Church, Martin Niemöller, and many of Dietrich's university students prepared brochures and posters for distribution at the
national church elections. Dietrich's parents loaned the use of
their home, car, and chauffeur to the effort. Dietrich and friends
worked day and night, writing and duplicating the brochures that
were then taken to the Young Reformers' offices in the Dahlem
section of Berlin. Somehow the Gestapo learned of their activities
and, on July 17, the Gestapo raided the headquarters and confiscated all the materials that Dietrich and the students had worked
so hard to create.

Dietrich was outraged. He and Jacobi stormed into Gestapo
headquarters and demanded to speak with the director, Rudolf
Diels. Dietrich argued with Diels over Hitler's promise to keep the
government out of church affairs. After Dietrich and Jacobi agreed
to some wording changes, Diels returned a few of the brochures.
Diels warned, though, that if Dietrich or Jacobi produced additional brochures or spread rumors insulting to the German Christians, they would be arrested.

When Dietrich's friends outside of Germany heard of the confrontation with the Gestapo, some believed that Dietrich had been
sent to a concentration camp. He responded, "I have not actually
been in a concentration camp, although, on the occasion of the
church election, the prospect of being sent there was held out to
me and my colleague by the highest police authority."[2]

Hitler and his advisors watched the church struggle closely. The
dissension within church circles gave them the excuse they

needed to declare that they would put an end to strife within the
church. Their interest had little to do with the welfare of the
church, but was a blatant move to place the German Christians in
the highest church offices and thereby gain control of the entire
German Evangelical Church. Because the Nazis controlled the
German Christians, they could essentially control the church.
Within a month, the entire structure of the German Evangelical
Church had changed. Elected bishops and superintendents were
suspended, and on July 23, in response to a plea from the German
Christians, particularly Ludwig Müller, Hitler gave a fifteen-
minute radio address focused on the church election. Hitler called
for "one united Reich Church" to take the place of "the multitude
of Protestant churches." He continued,

> In the interest of the renaissance of the German nation, which I
> regard as being inseparably bound up with the National Socialist
> movement, I therefore understandably want the new church elec-
> tions to result in support for our new national and state policy.

Hitler then announced, should the message have left any doubt,
that he put his trust in "these forces assembled in that sector of the
people of the Protestant church who as 'German Christians' have
deliberately trodden the ground of the National Socialist state."[3]

Despite the efforts of Dietrich and the other Young Reformers,
an overwhelming majority of German Christians gained key
church positions in the July elections. Not only were there inten-
tional irregularities in voter registration, but Hitler's July 23 radio
address gave a tremendous boost to the German Christians.
Hitler's speech was particularly devastating to the thousands of
Protestant pastors, including Martin Niemöller, a World War I vet-
eran, who had supported Hitler's plan to build a stronger Germany. These pastors had believed Hitler's earlier declarations to
leave the church alone.

Dietrich, however, had been skeptical from the beginning.
Dietrich and his students continued to work on behalf of the suspended church leaders and in opposition to the German Christian
Faith Movement. Dietrich and Franz Hildebrandt declared that
pastors must take a firm, decisive action as protest. They sug-

gested that all ministers should refuse to perform funeral services for as long as the government remained in control of church offices. Their ideas, however, were far too radical for most pastors, and their suggestion was ignored. Discouraged by the general lack of opposition, the two young men considered leaving the church. Soon after the election, Dietrich left Germany. It seemed impossible to resolve the issues facing the German church. In those decisive days of the struggle for the church, observers recalled that only Dietrich, Hildebrandt, Jacobi, and Martin Niemöller had been involved in every single event between May and July, attending meetings, issuing statements, organizing various kinds of publications. Niemöller, the oldest of the group and a well-respected member of the clergy, became the most recognized leader of the church struggle in the days leading up to World War II and immediately after.

The Young Reformers, at the urging of Martin Niemöller, decided that they must withdraw from politics and attempt to change the church's direction by writing a new confession, or statement of faith, for the German Evangelical Church. Further encouraged by Dietrich's mentor, Karl Barth, the Young Reformers commissioned Dietrich and theologian Hermann Sasse to write the confession.

Before beginning work on the confession, however, Dietrich went to London to interview for the position of pastor to two German-speaking congregations. Dietrich had been highly recommended for the job and several of his friends, Hermann Sasse among them, encouraged him to leave Germany. They feared for Dietrich's safety if he continued to openly oppose Hitler and challenge the Gestapo. The possibility of his being sent to a concentration camp was very real. Sasse said, "I saw in him one of Germany's best theologians and did not want to see him go under in the petty war against the Gestapo. . . ."[4]

Dietrich did not give an immediate answer to the German congregations in London who had invited him to come to England as their pastor. First he traveled to Bethel in northwestern Germany, not too far from the Dutch border. Bethel had been established in 1867 as a hospital for people suffering from epilepsy. It had grown over the years into a large Christian community with its own schools, churches, farms, and businesses. The care of the sick was still the main focus of activity, and the hospital included several buildings.

Dietrich had never visited Bethel before, and he was moved by what he observed there. He attended church services and saw people struck without warning by seizures so severe that no medication could prevent them. He saw the devoted nurses, both male and female, reach out to support the ill. For Dietrich the defenselessness of the epileptics paralleled the reality of human existence, "in which we are, in fact, basically helpless."[5] Later he would remember these courageous people when the Nazis began rounding up the disabled and taking them to concentration camps for "liquidation."

For most people in Germany at the time, of course, it was their own government, not disease, that threatened them. The sick and infirm, the Jews, communists, Gypsies, and Christians like Bonhoeffer who refused to pay allegiance to Hitler were all in danger of being seized by the government and imprisoned in concentration camps with barely a moment's notice. It was on March 22, 1933, that the first such camp, Dachau, opened. Located in a former munitions factory on the outskirts of Dachau, it was originally designed to hold political dissidents. It quickly shifted to a detention center for Jews, Gypsies, the disabled, homosexuals, Jehovah's Witnesses, and political opponents of Hitler. Common criminals were held there too, and eventually they all became part of the labor force used to produce armaments for Germany. Dachau was never designated as a death camp even after the "Final Solution," Hitler's plan to exterminate the Jews, became official policy, but hundreds of people died there. Most were shot supposedly trying to escape, and many more died from hunger, disease, physical exhaustion, or torture. For the patients at Bethel, however, the Nazi euthanasia program would pose a more immediate danger than the concentration camps.

The focus of Dietrich's time in Bethel was his work with Hermann Sasse writing the new confession. Despite the invigorating

Christian atmosphere at Bethel, Dietrich's task was a difficult one. He wrote to his grandmother:

> Our work here gives us much pleasure, but also much trouble. We want to try to make the German Christians declare their intentions. Whether we shall succeed I rather doubt. . . . The question really is: Germanism or Christianity? The sooner the conflict comes out into the open, the better.[6]

Called the Bethel Confession, it was finished in less than three weeks. Like Dietrich's lectures and sermons, the Bethel Confession issued a strong call for the church to remain true to the Bible. It presented a theological argument that recognized Israel as the Holy Land and the Jews as God's chosen people. Further it stated: "No nation can ever be commissioned to avenge on the Jews the murder [of Jesus] at Golgotha."[7] This confession is unique in that it included concern both for the Jews who had converted to Christianity (called Jewish Christians), as well as for those who had not. It recognized God's special favor on the Jewish people and put forward the obligation on the part of all Christians to face persecution themselves rather than to abandon the Jews. The completed confession was presented to a number of respected Protestant pastors and theologians.

As soon as he returned to Berlin, Dietrich joined with Martin Niemöller and with Franz Hildebrandt and Gerhard Jacobi to form the Pastors' Emergency League. The vows of the Pastors' Emergency League included a commitment to preach the Bible, to obey the confessions of the Reformation and to resist any attacks against them, to take responsibility for those who are persecuted, and to repudiate the Aryan Clause, which prohibited non-Aryans from taking civil service jobs. The Pastors' Emergency League anticipated that Hitler's government would apply the Aryan paragraphs to the clergy.

Niemöller sent a letter to all German pastors on September 12, 1933, inviting them to join the League. Thirteen hundred signed up immediately. By January 1934, 7,036 pastors had joined the cause. They stood in direct opposition to Hitler. At first Dietrich held out great hope that the German pastors in the Pastors' Emergency

League would show the kind of courage shown in 1941 by the pastors in Norway who gave up their pulpits rather than submit to Hitler's will.

Dietrich's decision to go to the London parishes reflected his disillusionment with the German church. He later wrote to Karl Barth:

> I was incomprehensibly in radical opposition to all my friends, that my views of matters were taking me more and more into isolation, although I was and remained in the closest personal relationship with these men—and all that made me anxious, made me uncertain. I was afraid I would go wrong out of obstinacy—and I saw no reason why I should see these things more correctly, better than so many able and good pastors, to whom I looked up—and so I thought that it was probably time to go into the wilderness for a while and simply do pastoral work, with as little demands as possible.[8]

He admitted that his disappointment that "the Bethel confession, on which I really worked so passionately, met with almost no understanding at all" was another factor in his decision. The future of the church in Germany looked particularly dreary to Dietrich, and he felt powerless to change its direction. The German Christian pastors had clearly given in to all of Hitler's demands and doctrines. They were intent on keeping the church alive at all costs, even if the church that survived no longer preached the Word of God.

The Catholic Church had also collapsed under Hitler's sway. Hitler's agents convinced the pope to sign a Concordat which guaranteed independence for Catholics in religious matters if the Catholic Church agreed not to interfere in political affairs. Despite the agreement a few brave priests continued actively to oppose Hitler and to speak out on behalf of the Jews.

Meanwhile the Bethel Confession had passed through the hands of twenty theologians. It was so changed and altered from its original form that Dietrich refused to sign it. Discouraged by the state of the church in Germany and feeling abandoned by his own colleagues, Dietrich accepted the offer of the London congregations and made plans to leave Germany.

Before going to London, Dietrich attended the World Alliance of Churches meeting in Sofia, Bulgaria. He worked both in open sessions and in private meetings to press the Alliance to respond to the problems in Germany. One of those in attendance at a small private meeting wrote in his diary:

> In Sofia, Bonhoeffer was able to inform us in a private group . . . about the real situation in Germany and of the brutal and intransigent attitude of the German Christians. We closed with prayer together. Bonhoeffer was very moved.[9]

A resolution on the issue approved by the World Alliance was largely the result of Dietrich's prompting. It directly addressed the treatment of German Jews: "We especially deplore the fact that the state measures against Jews in Germany have had such an effect on public opinion in some circles that the Jewish race is considered a race of inferior status."[10] The resolution was a clear indication of the opposition to Hitler forming outside of Germany. While the reference to Jews as a "racial group" may be offensive to twenty-first-century readers, the statement should be seen as a bold initiative inspired by Dietrich's reports.

In spite of all the hard work at the conference, Dietrich found time to wander around the exotic markets of Bulgaria and purchase some antiques. He returned to Berlin for another round of church meetings and farewell parties with his Berlin students. Dietrich was sorry to leave the Berlin students, many of whom had become his friends, but he felt keenly the need to escape from Germany for a period of quiet reflection.

10

England

1933–1935

A S IT TURNED OUT, Dietrich's time in London proved anything but quiet. He arrived in London on October 17, 1933, and moved into a home provided by his congregations. It was a large house, drafty and poorly heated. Dietrich lived on the second floor; the first was used by a German school. His parents kept in close contact with him by phone, and when they realized how barren his rooms were, they sent him a grand piano and some bulky furniture and hired a housekeeper for him. Soon after he arrived, Dietrich bought a young St. Bernard puppy and set about training it. He was quite sad when the St. Bernard was killed by a car in London.

Dietrich had hoped that his friend Franz Hildebrandt would also be able to serve a church in England, but Franz did not find a position. Dietrich invited him to share his rooms with him, and Franz ended up staying three months. Both men were excellent pianists, and although they disagreed over theological issues and often argued long into the night, music always brought a happy resolution to their arguments. They always agreed, however, on the need for the churches in Germany to wrest control from the German Christians and to oppose Hitler's policies.

Another friend from Berlin, Wolf-Dieter Zimmermann, also

stayed with Dietrich for a while. He recalled that the three friends slept late, ate breakfast around 11:00 A.M., and read the *London Times* to learn the latest news from Germany before each went off to work. In the evenings, they met again for theological conversations, music, or outings to movies or the theater. They usually stayed up talking or telling stories until two or three in the morning. According to Zimmermann, Dietrich and Franz were living in a state of permanent dispute. Their arguing was continual, interrupted only by laughter and music. Both men felt that such intellectual debate sharpened their own thinking, and, despite its rigor, it was never acrimonious. In fact, Franz delighted in telling how Dietrich teased him. Hildebrandt biographers Amos Cresswell and Maxwell Tow, included an example of such teasing:

> Sometimes when they were both involved in an argument Franz would produce his trump card, his clinching point. At this moment Dietrich would look up and say "What was that? I'm sorry I didn't hear a word." Then, as Franz said, "even the best rejoinder falls a little flat when it is repeated a second time." So they would usually dissolve into laughter.[1]

In addition to these two friends, many of Dietrich's students from Berlin visited him in London, as did his sisters and their husbands. His rooms also became the meeting place for his church youth groups, who came to listen to music, rehearse a nativity play, or simply to have interesting conversations. Dietrich enjoyed serving the two small congregations.

The congregation at Sydenham numbered between thirty and forty. The congregation at St. Paul's was only slightly larger. Because neither church alone could afford a minister, they joined together to hire one who would serve both churches. Dietrich was kept quite busy tending to the needs of two church programs, writing sermons, visiting the sick, and working with the growing number of German refugees who were arriving daily in England. Actions against Jews increased and hundreds of thousands of Jews left the country. Dietrich met many of these German refugees in London, and his churches tried to help in the resettlement. Often, however, the Jews were no more welcome outside of Germany than they were within Germany's borders.

The refugees served as a constant reminder of what was happening in Germany. British Consul-General R. T. Smallbones reported anti-Semitic activities that he had witnessed in Frankfurt on May 28. "On the windows of Jews' shops . . . various caricatures of Jews were painted, such as Jews hanging from gibbets, with insulting inscriptions."[2] Jews were warned to leave Germany quickly before something far worse than a boycott happened. Earlier that same May of 1933 books that were considered "un-German" or foreign, especially books by Jewish authors and scholars, were gathered from libraries and bookstores by members of the German Student Union. Special ceremonies featured speeches honoring Nazi ideals and ended with the burning of the books. No precise count is available of the number of books burned, but some experts estimate that over one hundred million books were destroyed in twelve years of Nazi supremacy. A hundred years earlier German poet Heinrich Heine had warned, "Where books are burned, they will ultimately also burn human beings." On hearing of the 1933 book burnings, Sigmund Freud is quoted as saying, "Only our books? In earlier times they would have burned us with them."[3]

Germany was always in Dietrich's mind. He read the news, sought out anyone who was traveling to or from Berlin, and called home so often that the phone company reduced his telephone bill out of compassion. The news from home was discouraging. The power of the German Christians and their allegiance to Hitler continued to grow. One leader of the German Christians went so far as to propose that the church should eliminate the Old Testament from the Bible, name Germany the Holy Land, and declare that Jesus was a German. His speech caused such outrage that the German Christians pulled back, but it was only a temporary defeat. Dietrich's own experiences as a child playing with the sons and daughters of Jewish professors and doctors allowed him to see Hitler's propaganda for the lie that it was. The Bonhoeffer parents had never tolerated prejudice. As a student Dietrich had become aware that many of Germany's greatest composers, musicians, writers, scientists, doctors, and thinkers were Jewish. Hitler, however, played on a deep-seated German anti-Semitism to turn neighbor against neighbor. From abroad, Dietrich watched the escalation of words and actions against the Jews and feared for his neighbors, friends, and family.

Dietrich waited a few weeks after his arrival in England to let Karl Barth know of his move. He feared that Barth would try to persuade him to return to Germany, and he was right. Barth answered Dietrich's letter with a command that he return to Germany by the next ship. Despite Barth's reservations about Dietrich's move to London, the decision turned out to be a good one. Dietrich made friends with George Bell, bishop of Chichester, a powerful church official in England. The bishop introduced Dietrich to other British church leaders and politicians and proved in later years to be a strong supporter of those Germans who opposed Hitler. With Bishop Bell's encouragement, Dietrich wrote articles about the situation in Germany for several British journals and gave interviews to a number of newspaper reporters. Bell himself had been asked to write an article on the German church, but he deferred to Dietrich, saying to the journal's editors, "I should however like to suggest a man who would do the article with great ability and first-hand knowledge."[4] He went on to describe Dietrich as someone who speaks English perfectly, is in daily contact with Berlin, and was the first to sign the "manifesto" of the Pastors' Emergency League. Bell's admiration for the young German theologian was obvious. Dietrich met frequently with Bell to update him on events in Germany and worked with the other German pastors in England to gain their support for the Pastors' Emergency League. He also traveled to Germany frequently to confer with Martin Niemöller and the other members of the Pastors' Emergency League.

In October of 1934, Hitler withdrew Germany from the League of Nations. This move was extremely popular, especially as Hitler's withdrawal also included the planned Disarmament Conference. Martin Niemöller joined in sending Hitler a telegram that pledged support in the name of "2,500 Evangelical pastors who do not belong to the German Christian Faith movement, we pledge our true support and prayerful thoughts."[5] Both Dietrich and Franz Hildebrandt were shocked by the telegram. Hildebrandt wrote to Niemöller, "I find it impossible to understand how you can joyfully welcome the political move in Geneva. . . ."[6] The two young pastors were in almost constant contact with Niemöller by letter, telegram, and telephone, giving him advice and confronting him about the stand that he was taking on behalf of the Pastors' Emergency League.

A vote on November 12 endorsed Hitler's decision, and the following evening over twenty thousand German Christians rallied at the Sportspalast in Berlin to celebrate. The rally, organized by German Christian leader Reinhold Krause, ended in protests, not only from the Pastors' Emergency League but even from some German Christians. Krause had gone too far in his comments, saying that the state church must liberate itself "from the Old Testament with its Jewish money morality and from these stories of cattle dealers and pimps."[7] He called for the immediate application of the Aryan Clause to the Protestant clergy. Reaction was so strong against Krause's comments, that the Aryan Clause was temporarily suspended. By this time, Franz Hildebrandt had returned to Berlin to help Martin Niemöller, and he kept Dietrich posted by telephone. They no longer could depend on newspaper reports because of the distortion of the press for propaganda purposes. Dietrich frequently returned to Berlin to visit family and to meet with Niemöller, Hildebrandt, and others active in the church struggle. He would then return to London with the latest news and rally support there.

In January of 1934 the German Christian bishop of the Evangelical Church issued a decree that forbade ministers from including in their sermons anything related to the intensifying church struggles. Sometimes when two pastors served a single congregation, one would be a German Christian and the other a member of the Pastors' Emergency League. There are recorded instances of physical fights for control of the pulpit with church members shoving one pastor into the pulpit while dragging another out. Most of the church struggles were not this dramatic, of course, but emotions were running high.

The Pastors' Emergency League immediately drew up a protest statement against the church edict banning discussion of the church struggles. Nearly four thousand pastors courageously read the protest the following Sunday even though they could have been jailed for such an act of rebellion. The widespread protest drew Hitler's attention. He called the church leaders to a conference in his office on January 26. Martin Niemöller spoke for the Pastors' Emergency League. Hitler told Niemöller that the pastors should leave the care of the Third Reich to him and confine their concerns to the church. While there are various accounts of Niemöller's response, one reports that Niemöller said, "But we too as Christians have a duty and neither you nor any power in the world is in the position to take it away from us."[8]

Hitler never forgave Niemöller. The Dahlem pastor's home was searched that very evening. A few days later a homemade bomb exploded in Niemöller's house, and he was eventually imprisoned by the Gestapo for eight years as the "personal prisoner of the Führer."

Niemöller was not the only one challenged by the Gestapo. In the spring of 1934, seven pastors were placed on trial in Mecklenburg for their protest activities. The three main defendants were sentenced to three, four, and six months in prison. Others also protested; Pastor Paul Schneider endured three arrests and detainment in Buchenwald before his eventual murder in 1939 at the hands of his captors. In January 1934 the Pastors' Emergency League numbered over 7,000 pastors, but the number dropped rapidly to 5,226 by 1936 as pressure on the churches grew.

The last effort of the Pastors' Emergency League to save the German Evangelical Church resulted in one of the great Christian declarations of faith, the Barmen Confession, written in large part by Dietrich's mentor, Karl Barth. The Barmen Confession spoke directly to the German Christians' apparent willingness to accept Hitler's word as equal to that of God and the Nazi swastika as equal to the cross of Christ.

The Barmen Confession was followed by the founding of a new church group in Germany, the Confessing Church. This group, formed by those who had been part of the Pastors' Emergency League, separated itself from the German Christians and therefore from the state church of Germany, the German Evangelical

Church. Dietrich fully supported the Confessing Church and was eventually summoned home from London to head one of the Confessing Church's seminaries to train young pastors.

Before going home, though, Dietrich attended another World Alliance Conference in Fanö, Denmark. Dietrich fought successfully to gain a place at the conference for the representatives from the Confessing Church. He gave a lecture and preached at morning service. According to Otto Dudzus, a student and colleague of Dietrich's, the August 28 sermon left his audience breathless. Dietrich said that Christians "may not use weapons against one another because they know that in so doing they are aiming those weapons at Christ himself." It was a strong call for peace. Dietrich challenged his listeners, representatives of Christian churches throughout the world, to

> send out to all believers this radical call to peace. . . . The hour is late. The world is choked with weapons, and dreadful is the distrust which looks out of all men's eyes. The trumpets of war may blow tomorrow. For what are we waiting?[9]

Commenting on the sermon years later, Otto Dudzus, who heard the speech wrote:

> This passionate call to a world Church which feels itself responsible for peace was for Bonhoeffer not an isolated affair which was broken off because it obviously found no echo. He stuck to this responsibility throughout all the complications and confusions, including his personal "change" from a pacifist to an active resistance fighter.[10]

Although the conference delegates focused on the problems of the church in Germany, they did not expand their consideration to the inevitable approach of war. Dietrich was elected to an ecumenical committee on Practical Christianity, called "Life and Work," and he continued his involvement with ecumenical work over the next several years. Dietrich took the work of the Fanö conference seriously (he had prepared for it for months in England), but once there, he thoroughly enjoyed himself, visiting with friends and swimming in the chilly North Sea.

The idea of going to India and learning about Gandhi's method of passive resistance remained attractive to Dietrich. Through his friendship with Bishop Bell he received an invitation directly from Gandhi to spend time at his *ashram* and to accompany him as he journeyed through India. Karl Barth heard of the plans and wrote Dietrich to express his disapproval:

> . . . the only thing I've heard about you in ages is the strange news that you intend to go to India so as to learn some kind of spiritual technique from Gandhi or some other holy man and that you expect great things of its application in the West.[11]

Barth was not the only one who thought Dietrich's fascination with Gandhi peculiar. His friends Gerhard Jacobi and Franz Hildebrandt also discouraged the journey. Dietrich was curious to find out if Gandhi represented God's will for nations. Could passive resistance bring about peace? He was also interested in Gandhi's response to suffering. As Dietrich had suggested in the Bethel Confession, Gandhi took seriously the idea that it is better to suffer for others than to live by force and coercion. In the end, it was the urgent call to head a Confessing Church seminary that made Dietrich choose Berlin over India. Confessing Church leaders realized that since the German Christians controlled all the official seminaries, the Confessing Church must begin training its own pastors if it was to survive. Before returning to Germany as a seminary director, Dietrich toured several seminaries and religious communities in England.

11

Finkenwalde

T HE SEMINARIES that Dietrich visited in England were well-established institutions with impressive buildings, adequate supplies, and large faculties. The new Confessing Church seminary at Zingst was a very poor, distantly related cousin. The Confessing Church, unlike the English churches, had few funds to help cover the cost of running seminaries or hiring ministers. The new seminary had no building, no faculty, no established curriculum. In fact, the first class met in an old church conference center on the Baltic Sea with Dietrich and his assistant, Wilhelm Rott, as the only teachers. There was a rundown building surrounded by small, unheated cabins dotted among the sand dunes. The twenty-three students (called *ordinands* because they were preparing for ordination as pastors) gathered in the main building for classes. If the weather was nice, they gathered on the sandy shore for discussion or singing. From the start, Dietrich encouraged the young ministers to find time to play. They swam in the sea, played tennis, or went for walks in the nearby forests during the lovely summer days. While this made for an idyllic setting in summer, the approach of winter forced the seminary to move to heated quarters after only a few short weeks.

For ten days the ordinands stayed in a youth hostel while

Dietrich and Wilhelm Rott found a more permanent location. An old estate in Finkenwalde, which had served as a private school, seemed the perfect choice. A gymnasium and extra classrooms had been added to the old house. When the ordinands arrived at the schoolhouse, they found it almost empty. Dietrich divided them into teams: some to begin a garden, some to clean and paint the rooms, others to ask friends of the Confessing Church for any furniture or food they could spare. Generous contributions poured in: cartloads of furniture, farm produce, and even two grand pianos from sympathetic church members. Such contributions were essential to the running of the seminary. The Confessing Church had very little money to spend on the seminaries. Over the years, the neighboring farmers contributed vegetables, fruits, and even meat. One day the phone rang and Dietrich was told that a live pig had been dropped off at the seminary. There was always a shortage of books for the ordinands, so Dietrich contributed his entire personal library to the seminary, including reference books, Bible commentaries, theological books, and books on church history.

There was no shortage of music, however. In addition to the two grand pianos, many students brought their own instruments. Dietrich himself had learned to play the guitar and used it to accompany singing when students gathered in the woods or on the beach. He also brought along his phonograph and his collection of records, including the Negro spirituals he collected in New York. The students often formed impromptu orchestras or gathered around the phonograph to join in singing "Swing Low, Sweet Chariot."

Eberhard Bethge was a member of the first class at the new seminary. Born on August 28, 1909, Eberhard, the son of a Lutheran pastor, had watched as the villagers sought his father's wise counsel. This made such a lasting impression that he decided that he too would become a pastor. He never questioned this decision even during the difficult days of the church struggle. What he did question was the Nazification of the church. Eberhard, along with fifteen other candidates for the ministry who were active in the Young Reformers movement, was expelled from the German

Evangelical seminary in Wittenberg for refusing to sign an oath of
allegiance to the Reich bishop. They felt that Reich Bishop Müller
and the German Christians were taking the church in the wrong
direction, but they, like most German clergy, did not yet recognize
where Hitler's anti-Semitic measures would ultimately lead. The
call of the day was "Let the church be the church," and behind this
was the understanding that the church should remain apolitical.

The Confessing Church leaders welcomed the theology students and assigned several, including Eberhard, to the seminary
at Zingst. Many of the ordinands in the first classes at Finkenwalde had been Dietrich's students in Berlin. Other students, such
as Eberhard Bethge, came to Finkenwalde after being expelled by
the German Christians from the established seminaries because
they refused to give their allegiance to Hitler.

Eberhard Bethge had never heard of Dietrich Bonhoeffer. Many
years later, Eberhard described that first meeting:

> I turned up in the evening, a day later than the others, and I looked
> around to find out who the director was. He was barely distin-
> guishable as such. Most of us were almost the same age as he was,
> so someone had to point him out. He came to greet me, and to my
> amazement invited me to go for a walk along the beach with him.
> As we walked up and down he asked me what I had gone through
> so far in the church struggle, where I came from, and about my
> family and friends. This taking a personal interest from the start
> was quite new to me, as compared to the theological teachers I had
> met before.[1]

Eberhard discovered that Dietrich was only three years his senior,
enjoyed sports but hated to lose at games, and was a gifted pianist.
He described Dietrich as "a powerful man." Bethge noticed that
Dietrich was "a tall, powerfully built man of hardly thirty years,
with lively blue eyes, a sensitive but controlled mouth, and rather
relaxed movements. He revealed himself to be an extremely
unconventional guide to this collection of aspiring ministers. . . .
Only very reluctantly and very rarely did he allow himself to lose
in the games we played on the shore. . . ."[2] Dietrich walked at a
brisk pace, and he tended to talk fast, unless he was preaching,
when his speech became slower and carefully measured. His

warm, friendly smile reassured students that this seminary director was not only a serious scholar but was someone who enjoyed
a good laugh. Dietrich's students and friends delighted in his
sense of humor.

Only four or five days after their meeting, Eberhard learned
how his teacher felt about the Hitler regime. The students were listening to the radio when Hitler referred to universal military service (mandated on May 16, 1935). Dietrich reacted with total
disapproval. For the German ordinands, who had been raised to
be strong nationalists, this was a surprising reaction. Later that
evening, Dietrich calmly explained to the students his beliefs
about pacifism and how it related to Christ's teaching in the
Sermon on the Mount. Although not all the students accepted
Dietrich's beliefs as their own, they all listened and pondered this
very un-German teaching. As Eberhard later recalled, "He spoke
without any fanaticism, but we were amazed, as we had never
been taught like that in our whole course of studies."[3]

In the early days at Finkenwalde, Eberhard Bethge was no hap-
pier than the other ordinands with the daily schedule that Dietrich
proposed. The day began with a half hour of common worship,
which included Bible readings, music, and prayers. Immediately
after breakfast, the ordinands were expected to meditate for half
an hour in silence on a single passage of ten to fifteen verses of
Scripture. They focused on the same reading for an entire week.
After the meditation, they attended classes, ate lunch, and relaxed
with games (which included swimming in summer or skating in
winter) before additional classes. After supper each evening, they
all joined together again for music, indoor games, or reading
aloud. Just before bed, there was another half-hour prayer service.
Dietrich asked that they remain silent until breakfast the next
morning.

Some of the ordinands found the schedule too strict, and all of
them complained about the half hour of silent meditation. Some
wanted to smoke, others to read, others to polish their shoes.
What if their minds wandered? How could they focus on one
Bible passage for an entire half hour?

Dietrich listened patiently to their complaints, but did not relent. The discipline of daily meditation was important, he said, and he showed them by his own stillness and concentration what it meant. The meditation proved to be a great help when they were writing sermons, and in the years to follow, when many of the young pastors were in prison, the discipline of this meditation provided them with great comfort and a living connection to their fellow students, whom they came to call "brothers," at Finkenwalde.

There was one rule that Dietrich insisted upon: no one was to speak about another person in that person's absence. Gossip was not allowed. If such a mistake was made, it was necessary to inform the absent brother at the first possible opportunity. The ordinands learned much from observing—and breaking—this rule.

On one Saturday night before Sunday's communion service, Dietrich called the students together and suggested that in order to be truly free, they must be willing to confess any resentments toward anyone else. He suggested that each person choose one other as his confessor and prayer partner. One student wrote of the experience:

> We went to see one another and spoke of many grievances stored up in the last few weeks. It was a great surprise to realize how we had hurt the other person, without intention, by chance. . . . Now we knew what it meant to consider other people.[4]

Many close relationships were established in this way among the students, and these relationships continued to provide support even after the men were separated by distant parishes, prison, or active military service. Knowing that someone was remembering them in prayer helped to dispel the sense of loneliness. Several of the students chose Dietrich as their confessor. Dietrich chose Eberhard Bethge.

Eberhard was a man worthy of such trust. He had already completed his theological training and was conversant with the works of Karl Barth. Dietrich recognized in Eberhard a faithful, trustworthy, and intelligent young man fully committed to the church of Jesus Christ. In the years to come, Eberhard's gentle but perceptive questions would help Dietrich to focus his thoughts as he worked out difficult ethical and spiritual issues. Dietrich Bonhoeffer and Eberhard Bethge developed one of the most remarkable friendships in the history of the church.

The purpose of the seminary was to prepare theological students for the practical work of parish ministry. Dietrich taught courses on sermon writing, for example, and he designed opportunities for the students to preach in nearby churches. As in his university classes, Dietrich taught by asking questions and guiding discussion. His strongest form of instruction, however, was by example. Eberhard Bethge tells of an incident on the second day of the first seminary course when the housekeeper asked for some help cleaning up the supper dishes. No one volunteered. "Without saying a word Bonhoeffer rose from the table, disappeared into the kitchen and refused to let in the others who hurried to follow him. Afterward he rejoined the students on the beach, but he made no comment."[5]

In a similar manner, Dietrich carried soup to a student too sick with flu to leave his bed, quietly arranged hospital care for a student recovering from surgery, and tried in every way to serve his students by following Christ's example of service to others. Dietrich cared deeply for his students; they were the future of the Confessing Church, and they were taking a dangerous course by entering the ministry in opposition to the German Christians and the Nazi government. He also understood the practical resources they would need not only for their life in the parish but also for their own spiritual life. Preaching was a priority, and he provided his students with advice. He taught them to relax, even when it came to preparing sermons, and therefore to write during the day and in short bursts, not in one long sustained period. He encouraged them to use the first few minutes of the sermon when the congregation is alert and ready to hear the most important words, and he stressed that the essential function of the sermon is to testify to the Word of God.

Prayer, too, was something he felt should be taught and learned. His own prayers followed a distinct pattern. Eberhard Bethge describes the prayers at Finkenwalde as beginning with a detailed word of thanks for the many gifts of God, both spiritual and practical, followed by a plea for tolerance and understanding among the brothers. There were prayers for the Confessing Church and its pastors, for those in prison, for those who were enemies. Dietrich prepared his prayers carefully, uplifting particular themes of the day, but using the Psalms as a model.

Each course of study at Finkenwalde lasted for three or four months. Even before the first course was over, Dietrich made a startling proposal to the governing body of the Confessing Church. He proposed the establishment of a House of Brethren at Finkenwalde where six young pastors would live together and assist in the duties of running the seminary. They would also help with mission work in the local churches. Dietrich believed that such a Christian community would strengthen the seminary. In his letter to the governing board of the Confessing Church, he said that the ordinands at the seminary needed to learn two things. First they must learn to live in community with one another, sharing an obedience to the will of Christ and understanding the strength they would find as they served one another. The House of Brethren was to help create and expand this sense of Christian community. Eberhard Bethge was among the first group to participate in this bold new experiment in communal living.

Dietrich wrote that the second task of the seminary was his responsibility. The ordinands must come to appreciate the truth of Scripture in their lives and in their duties as pastors. This Dietrich taught by both his words and his deeds. All the students agreed that the greatest strength and power for truth at Finkenwalde was Dietrich himself. Although he was extremely reserved, everyone who spoke with him felt the magnetism of his personality. He continued to inspire his students to great courage, and later, when he was in prison, his very presence gave comfort and courage to those around him. One man who served time in prison with Dietrich later said that Dietrich exuded confidence and that it was impossible to be a coward when he was present.

Dietrich traveled to Berlin frequently because he was still lecturing at the university and he needed to meet with the governing councils of the Confessing Church. He also attended ecumenical meetings in England, visited family, and learned the latest news of Hitler's military and social attacks. Whenever Dietrich returned from these visits, the students gathered around him eager for news of the church struggle. In September of 1935 he reported the departure of Karl Barth for his native Switzerland after Barth refused to take an oath of allegiance to Hitler and that a series of new Emergency Measures had been set up to destroy the Confessing Church. S.S. leader Heinrich Himmler was instrumental in passing and enforcing these measures, which had the effect of cutting state funds to Confessing ministers and seminaries.

When the first course ended, most of the ordinands returned to their home churches. They were ordained, but because of the church conflict, they were labeled "illegal pastors." They would have no recognition by the state church and therefore no salary. They would depend on the free-will offering of a congregation and the protection of a local bishop who agreed with the beliefs of the Confessing Church. Some, finding no church open to them, tried to set up small congregations of believers in private homes, but this proved to be especially dangerous. Gestapo interrogation, threats, and concentration camp imprisonment awaited many if not all of them.

The last of the Emergency Measures, passed in December 1935, prohibited unauthorized groups from performing ecclesiastical functions. This was certainly aimed at the Confessing Church and had the effect of making their seminaries illegal. The Confessing Church Councils were forbidden to appoint clergy to church posts, to ordain new ministers, to assemble in synod meetings, or to train ministers. Any monies collected during church services had to be returned to the state. When Dietrich broke the news to his students, not a single one left the seminary even though they all understood the dangers imposed by their decision to stay. They were liable to arrest and imprisonment for defying the Emergency Measures, and their chance of obtaining a paying position as pastor was slim, if not impossible. The young pastors desperately needed courage. Once the Emergency Measures took effect, large numbers of the illegal pastors were arrested.

A continuing problem was the lack of clear-cut organization in the Confessing Church. There was neither constitution nor ordinances typical of German church administration. The Confessing Church never separated itself structurally from the German Evangelical Church. The seminary in Finkenwalde was only one of several set up to train ministers. Although the Finkenwalde seminary took in only male ordinands, several of the seminaries included both men and women. In some parts of Germany, the Confessing congregations continued to receive monies from the state church tax; in other areas, there were few if any funds to keep the churches and seminaries running.

Finkenwalde received extraordinary support from many of the landed families of Pomerania. One special friend, Ruth von Kleist-Retzow, was an older woman who took an interest in Dietrich's writings and pledged her support to him and his students. Dietrich was often a guest in her home, and she frequently attended services at Finkenwalde, sometimes bringing along her grandchildren. In times of trouble, one or another of Dietrich's former students or their wives stayed on the von Kleist-Retzow estate, gradually regaining strength for the church struggles ahead. Her support included funding, but also a level of concern and comfort that renewed both Bonhoeffer and his students. As Werner Koch, one of the first students at Finkenwalde, wrote, "she loved the Confessing Church, and was ever watchful of the dangers which might threaten it from within and without."[6] She became extremely close to Dietrich, read all of his theological writing, invited him to teach confirmation to her many grandchildren, and protected him for as long as it was possible. One of Ruth von Kleist-Retzow's granddaughters, Maria von Wedemeyer, eventually became Dietrich's fiancée.

12

Protests and
Persecution

1936-1937

EVEN THOUGH FINKENWALDE was far from Berlin, neither
Dietrich nor the ordinands were removed from the church
struggle. A frequent topic of discussion both at the seminary
and among parish pastors was the interpretation of Christ's teaching. What exactly did the words of Romans 13 mean for Christians
in Germany? This verse teaches that all authority comes from
God. "Therefore whoever resists authority resists what God has
appointed, and those who resist will incur judgment." Did this
mean that Hitler's authority was God-given? The German Christians used this verse and the teachings of Martin Luther to justify
their subservience to Hitler. Martin Luther, founder of the
Lutheran Church, had strongly supported the relationship
between church and state in his writing. How should the Confessing Church pastors interpret this verse four hundred years
after Luther? Could they challenge the essence of German theological thought? Dietrich taught his students by asking such questions and encouraging a give-and-take kind of discussion among
his students assuring them that "even an answer or a question
that seemed silly might be of use."[1]

It was clear, though, from his teaching and preaching that he
had no ambivalence about the relationship between state and

church. He was, after all, the man who had suggested active political resistance as early as 1933. In an April 1936 lecture to the
students at Finkenwalde he outlined the problem facing congregations when the church leadership was divided into three camps:
the German Christians, the Confessing Church, and those who
remained neutral. He said that it was the responsibility of the
Confessing Church to establish emergency ministries in churches
where the German Christians held control. Congregations were
confused, Dietrich said, and it was the obligation of the Confessing Church to provide guidance. In an oft-quoted statement, he
declared that "whoever separate the question of the Confessing
church from the question of their own salvation do not understand that the struggle of the Confessing Church is the struggle for
their own salvation. . . . "[2]

In February 1936, even before the Emergency Measures took
effect, the Confessing Church council wrote to students saying:

> The time has now come for you to make your decision. . . . We can
> give no guarantee that you will find employment, that you will
> receive a stipend, or that you will be recognized by any state
> authority. We neither want nor are entitled to conceal this from you.
> It is likely that your path from now on will be very hard. . . .[3]

Dietrich mentioned the names of all those who had been arrested
or were under restrictions during morning and evening prayer
services. He wrote letters to former Finkenwalde students, and he
visited those in prison whenever that was possible. One of the
special tasks of the House of Brethren was to provide additional
support for those in jail, as well as for former students who had
been sent to distant and lonely parishes. They not only visited as
many of the small parishes as possible, but wrote letters of support, which they called "circular letters" because the letter traveled in a circle from one former student to the next until all had
received it. The letters included news of fellow students, a brief
discussion of a particular theological problem, and a list of Bible
texts for meditation. Even though they were separated by space
and circumstance, the young pastors felt a sense of companion-
ship, knowing that all of their Christian brothers were meditating

on the same text. Sending the letters was illegal, but Dietrich felt that the letters were essential to the morale of the young pastors.

Dietrich's students helped him to celebrate his thirtieth birthday on February 4, 1936. After much singing and storytelling, the students asked if they might have a birthday wish. Would Dietrich help them organize a visit to Sweden?

Dietrich agreed, and in very short time he arranged for the entire seminary (twenty-three students and their teachers) to travel to Copenhagen and then on to Sweden. The Swedish church officials not only paid the cost of the ten-day visit, but they provided encouragement for those involved in the church struggle. In return, the Swedish officials received firsthand knowledge about the problems facing the Confessing Church in Germany.

The visit did not escape the notice of the German Christian Bishop for Foreign Affairs. He labeled Dietrich a pacifist and enemy of the state. He recommended that Dietrich no longer be allowed to train German seminary students. While the bishop could not stop Dietrich's work at the seminary, which was already considered illegal, he did manage to prevent Dietrich from lecturing at Berlin University. Dietrich gave his final lecture at the university on February 14, 1936, and then focused his full attention on Finkenwalde seminary and the rapidly deteriorating condition of the Confessing Church.

As the conflict between the Nazi government and the Confessing Church increased, so did the pressures within the Confessing Church. Dietrich never wavered in his belief that the church must remain the church of Jesus Christ and must not accept the false teaching of Hitler and the Nazis. He continued to speak out against Hitler's treatment of the Jews and against Hitler himself. He said on one occasion:

> If I see that a madman is driving a car into a group of innocent bystanders, I as a Christian cannot simply wait for the catastrophe and cover the wounded and bury the dead. I must wrest the steering wheel out of the hands of the driver.[4]

His statement initially made in a lecture at Finkenwalde that separation from the Confessing Church equals separation from salvation, perhaps more than any other, raised the cry of protest from his enemies, as well as from colleagues inside the Confessing Church. Dietrich ignored the storm of protest. Too much was at stake to be sidetracked by personal attacks.

Perhaps one of the most difficult moments came in early 1936 when a quiet but sincere student told Dietrich that he had decided to leave Finkenwalde. He had decided to follow the directives of the state church and pledge his allegiance to the Nazi regime. Dietrich talked with the student. Eberhard Bethge and the other members of the House of Brethren talked with the student, and so did his fellow ordinands. But, as Dietrich finally admitted, "Nothing we have been able to say has done any good." It was a sad day when the young man left Finkenwalde, but the brothers continued to include him in their prayers. Although he was not the last to leave the seminary and join the state church, the great majority of students remained faithful to the Confessing Church, which, as Dietrich said, carried the "responsibility of being . . . the true Church of Jesus."[5]

At Finkenwalde, Dietrich and the ordinands witnessed firsthand the result of oppression in the battered face of Pastor Sussbach, a young Christian minister with Jewish roots, who had been beaten up by the S.A. Dietrich brought the injured man to Finkenwalde to recover from his injuries. Two pastors from the small town of Seelow were arrested by the Gestapo because they refused to give up their churches to a German Christian pastor. They were both sent to a concentration camp. Once released, they too came to Finkenwalde to recover from their imprisonment.

Despite the increase in arrests and the increased persecution of Confessing Church pastors, Dietrich lived each day to the fullest. He played the piano and sang joyfully, joined the students in games, and took many long walks in the summer sunshine. Eberhard Bethge was always at his side, leading the students in singing, talking theology with Dietrich, and keeping track of various details related to seminary life and the increasing turmoil within the Confessing Church.

During the summer of 1936 the Olympics were held in Berlin. Hitler used the event to further his own cause. He spent twenty-five million dollars on Olympic facilities for the games, including nine new sports arenas. Over four thousand athletes from forty-nine nations participated. Hitler planned to use the Olympic Games to prove to the world that Germany was not only a strong and powerful nation, fully recovered from the losses of the First World War, but a Christian country as well. Although foreign visitors were impressed by what Hitler had accomplished, Dietrich and his students knew that the evils of the Nazi regime festered just outside the glittering domes of the arenas.

Dietrich traveled almost constantly between Berlin and Finken-walde. During the Olympics, in August 1936, the German Christians held daily lectures and church services for foreign visitors. The Confessing Church did likewise and, unlike the German Christians, their programs attracted large, overflow audiences. Dietrich was asked to speak, but did so reluctantly. The whole situation seemed explosive to Dietrich, and when the church group asked him to send a photograph for a propaganda brochure, he refused, saying that it was too late for the effort to have any significant effect. Everywhere he looked he saw signs that war was getting closer and closer. He urged calm and prayer.

While in Berlin, he spoke to an overflow crowd at St. Paul's Church. He gave a lecture, but wished that he could have preached a sermon instead. It was August 5, 1936, the last time he was to speak to a large public gathering. Soon his freedoms would be curtailed by the Gestapo, and he would be forbidden to speak, write, or even travel without special permission.

Always generous with his money and belongings, Dietrich purchased tickets to the Olympics for the ordinands and even bought plane tickets for two students who told him that they had always wanted to take an airplane ride. Dietrich seemed to get as much pleasure from this treat as the students did, possibly because pleasure amidst such disturbing events was a sweet reminder of better times.

At the end of August 1936 Dietrich and Eberhard attended an ecumenical conference in Chamby, Switzerland. After the conference they spent a few days touring Italy. Dietrich served as tour guide to Eberhard when they visited St. Peter's in Rome. It was a well-deserved break, one that Dietrich remembered fondly in his letters to Eberhard during his days in prison.

When Dietrich and Eberhard returned to Finkenwalde, they focused once again on the seminary students and on theological studies. Dietrich had begun a study of the Sermon on the Mount in 1932. In 1935–36 he completed it. The English edition of this book is called *The Cost of Discipleship*. It dispels the idea that it is easy to be a Christian. "Discipleship means allegiance to the suffering Christ, and it is therefore not at all surprising that Christians should be called upon to suffer."[6] Christians have become soft, Dietrich wrote, and expect to receive God's grace without being obedient to the teaching of God. God's grace, his love toward us, is costly. "Such grace is costly because it calls us to follow, and it is *grace* because it calls us to follow *Jesus Christ*. It is costly because it costs us our life, and it is grace because it give us the only true life."[7]

The book is based on Dietrich's close reading of the Sermon on the Mount (Matthew 5:1–11), and it gave voice to Dietrich's understanding that any attack on a child of God is a direct attack on God. Certainly his conversations with Jean Lasserre and his experiences in America influenced his writing, but this book, written in the midst of the church struggle, reflects not only his desire for peace, but his compassion for the persecuted. "Suffering," he wrote, "is the badge of true discipleship. . . . If we lose our life in his service and carry our cross, we shall find our lives again in the fellowship of the cross with Christ."[8] At the time he wrote *The Cost of Discipleship* he was in the midst of a great battle for the souls of the German people and the lives of their Jewish neighbors. *The Cost of Discipleship* was published in 1937 and is considered a classic statement on what it means to live a Christian life. In April of 2000, the editors of *Christianity Today* asked over one hundred of its contributors and church leaders to nominate the ten most important religious books of the twentieth century. *The Cost of Discipleship* was among the top choices.[9]

Dietrich traveled to Berlin as often as possible to meet with church leaders and to spend time with his family, enjoying music together or engaging in political conversations. Dietrich's sister Christine and her husband, Hans von Dohnanyi, lived in Berlin-Eichkamp, as did Dietrich's brother Klaus and his wife, Emmi. His youngest sister, Susi, lived in nearby Berlin-Dahlem, where her husband, Walter Dress, had taken over a pastorate. When Dietrich's mother turned sixty on December 30, 1936, the brothers and sisters and the fifteen grandchildren put on a musical performance of Haydn's *Toy Symphony*.

The party was held in the home that the Bonhoeffers had built in 1935. It was a large house designed with extra space for family gatherings, a small apartment for Dietrich's grandmother, Julie Bonhoeffer, and a spacious attic room for Dietrich. An extra bed was available for Eberhard, who often accompanied Dietrich to Berlin. The two friends constructed bookshelves along the back wall, and Dietrich placed his desk next to the window overlooking the house next door, which belonged to Dietrich's sister Ursula and her family. Dietrich, always an attentive uncle, tossed candies out his window to his nieces and nephews whenever he spied them in the gardens.

Back in Finkenwalde Dietrich continued his work with the ordinands. With the help of Eberhard Bethge and the members of the House of Brethren, Dietrich held reunions for former Finkenwalde students and continued his letter writing campaign to bolster their spirits and resolve. Gestapo surveillance of pastors increased—church meetings were interrupted by Gestapo visits; pastors were prohibited from speaking or were actually arrested (often as many as one hundred were in prison at the same time). They were usually released within a day or two. The Gestapo's primary intent was to scare them into obedience to the state, not to harm them.

On July 1, 1937, Dietrich and Eberhard traveled to Berlin to meet with Martin Niemöller. They had no idea that he had been arrested moments before their arrival. As they were visiting with Frau Niemöller, they saw the Gestapo arrive in several black Mercedes. They tried to escape quickly by the back door, but a Gestapo official met them there and herded them back inside. For seven hours they were kept under house arrest while the Gestapo officers searched every nook and cranny of Niemöller's house for evidence to use against him and the Confessing Church.

Dietrich's parents must have learned of the arrest because Dietrich caught sight of their car passing slowly by the Niemöllers' house several times during the day. When the search was over, Dietrich and Eberhard were allowed to return to Finkenwalde. Dietrich immediately sent a group of students to Berlin to participate in a demonstration outside of Niemöller's church, where Franz Hildebrandt, Dietrich's good friend, was now in charge.

Two weeks later Hildebrandt was also arrested by the Gestapo. His situation was far more dangerous than Martin Niemöller's because Hildebrandt's mother was Jewish. The Bonhoeffer family and other friends worked behind the scenes to secure Hildebrandt's release from prison, and since the Gestapo had not found his passport, he was able to travel to safety in England.

After Niemöller's arrest, persecution increased. Former Finkenwalde students reported that their homes were searched, their property was confiscated, and some of them were arrested. Dietrich wrote encouraging letters to the parents of the arrested pastors. He arranged for his friend, Ruth von Kleist-Retzow, to invite the wives of the arrested pastors to spend time at her country house. So many pastors had been arrested in the summer of 1937 that for a while it seemed as if all the pastors claiming allegiance to the Confessing Church would end up in prison. Over eight hundred clergymen were arrested in 1937, and so many others were subjected to threats, warnings, citations, and trials that they could not be counted. Despite all of the arrests during the last months of 1937, many of those arrested were freed by Christmas. Niemöller was not. He was to spend eight years as Hitler's personal prisoner. After the war, Niemöller was heralded as a hero. He became active in the World Council of Churches and toured the world. He visited the United States in 1947. When meeting with American church groups, he often spoke about the failure of the German churches to help the victims of Nazi persecution. During that tour, Niemöller is reported to have said,

When they arrested the Communists and socialists, I said: I am not Communist, so I did nothing. When they imprisoned the Jews, I said: I am not a Jew, so I did nothing. When they attacked the Catholics, I said: I am not a Catholic, so I did nothing. When they came for me, there was no one left.[10]

Dietrich would certainly have agreed with Niemöller's assessment of the church's impotence. In reality, however, Dietrich was still struggling to keep the church on track. He even tried to help Niemöller's family. He sent greetings to Niemöller's wife, Else, on her birthday and on Easter, and until his own arrest in 1942, he sent Christmas gifts to the Niemöller family. By 1938, the number of police measures taken against Protestant church workers was recorded as 4,468. This figure does not include those taken in for interrogation and released.

When the summer course ended, the students left, and Dietrich and Eberhard went on a brief visit to see Dietrich's sister Sabine and her family in Göttingen. While they was there, they received a phone call from the Finkenwalde housekeeper. The Gestapo had arrived, searched the house, and sealed its doors. Finkenwalde seminary was closed forever.

13

The Secret Seminaries

1937–1938

A CTION AGAINST THE JEWS was intensifying. Between 1933 and 1939 over three hundred thousand of Germany's five hundred thousand Jews left Germany for other countries. Leaving was difficult. Not only did those who left pay a heavy "security tax," but they were required to sign over to the government all their property. They took only a few personal belongings with them.

It was time for Dietrich's twin sister, Sabine, and her family to make a difficult decision. Her husband, Gerhard Leibholz, had been forced to retire from his teaching position in 1936 at the age of thirty-four. As a Jew, he could not find work, and while the large and generous Bonhoeffer family would have supported the Leibholz family, no one felt that Sabine's family would be safe in Berlin. The Bonhoeffers had learned, through their contacts within the Nazi government, that Jews would soon be required to have the letter "J" stamped in their passports. The borders would then be closed to any Jews trying to escape.

Plans were carefully and secretly made to allow the Leibholz family to escape from Germany. On September 8, 1938, Dietrich and Eberhard arrived at the Leibholz home in Göttingen. When the children, eleven-year-old Marianne and seven-year-old Christiane, awoke the next morning, their mother told them to prepare for a journey. Marianne remembers the morning clearly.

> I knew at once that something very serious was happening to us. . . . Our car was very full, but packed to look as if we were going on a normal holiday. Christiane and I were embedded in the back. Uncle Dietrich and "Uncle" Bethge had brought another car, Uncle Dietrich's, and intended to accompany us to the frontier, and during the drive my parents and uncles sat in the front seats of the two cars, changing places frequently, so that all came to sit with us children in turns.
>
> We stopped briefly in Göttingen where the men bought a giant torch [flashlight] for the journey. When we were out of town my mother said, "We're not going to Wiesbaden, we're trying to get across the Swiss border tonight. They may close the frontier because of the crisis."
>
> The roof of our car was open, the sky was deep blue, the countryside looked marvelous in the hot sunshine. I felt there was complete solidarity between the four grown-ups. I knew that unaccustomed things would be asked of us children from now on but felt proud of now being allowed to share the real troubles of the adults. I thought that if I could do nothing against the Nazis myself I must at the very least co-operate with the grown-ups who could. Christiane and I spent most of the time singing in the car, folk songs and rather militant songs about freedom, my mother, Uncle Dietrich, and "Uncle" Bethge singing with us. I enjoyed the various descants. Uncle Dietrich taught me a new round. . . .
>
> During the drive my uncle seemed to me just as I always remember him: very strong and confident, immensely kind, cheerful and firm.
>
> We stopped at Giessen and picnicked by the wayside. The grown-ups' mood did not strike me as depressing. Then all of a sudden they said it was getting late and that we must hurry. "We have to get across the frontier tonight, they may close it at any moment." We children settled in our car, our parents got in, and I remember Uncle Dietrich and "Uncle" Bethge waving farewell to us, until they became tiny and were cut off by a hill. The rest of the drive was no longer cheerful. My parents drove as fast as they could, we stopped talking so that they could concentrate. The atmosphere was tense.

We crossed the Swiss border late at night. Christiane and I pre-
tended to be asleep and very angry at being wakened, to discour-
age the German frontier guards from doing too much searching of
the car. My mother had put on a long, very brown suede jacket,
whose brownness was meant to pacify the German officials. They
let our car through and the Swiss let us in. My parents were not to
cross the German border again until after the war.[1]

Sabine and her family settled in England. Dietrich's friend, Bishop
George Bell, looked after Sabine's family and helped them get settled into a new country. It was difficult for the twins to be apart,
and although Dietrich did visit Sabine in 1939, communication
became extremely difficult and eventually impossible once the
war began.

Dietrich and Eberhard returned to Sabine's home in Göttingen,
where Dietrich began work on another book, *Life Together,* which
explained life in Finkenwalde's House of Brethren. The book was
written in only four weeks. While *The Cost of Discipleship* tried to
explain the meaning of the Christian life for the individual, *Life
Together* attempted to explain what it meant to live as a Christian
in a community with other Christians. Dietrich felt an urgency to
complete the project and to convince others that Finkenwalde had
not been a monastery, but a Christian community, always ready to
serve others. Word about Dietrich's experiment in communal living had spread throughout the Confessing Church, and people
were eager to find out more about the House of Brethren. Dietrich
was hesitant to publicize his work at Finkenwalde too soon, but
with the premature closing of the House of Brethren he felt the
need to record the results of his experiment. "The physical presence of other Christians," he wrote, "is a source of incomparable
joy and strength to the believer."[2] *Life Together* was published in
1939 and immediately attracted readers.

Although there was no chance of reopening Finkenwalde, the
Confessing Church felt a great need to continue training pastors.
Dietrich, Eberhard, and other Confessing Church leaders believed
that at no time in recent history had the German people faced such
a need for church leaders dedicated to preaching the Bible and to
following the traditional confessions of the Christian church.

Many pastors had been forced into the army. Many others had turned away from God's teachings of brotherly love and compassion when they accepted the terms offered by Adolf Hitler and the German Christians.

A new plan developed to hide the seminaries from the Gestapo by assigning students to two separate parishes as for training. The students registered with the Gestapo as required, and then met in secret groups of eight to ten for training. Dietrich and Eberhard returned to the countryside near Stettin to form another illegal seminary. This time there was no one building, but two "collective pastorates" forty miles apart in the towns of Koslin and Schlawe. At least twice each week Dietrich traveled between the two, instructing the ordinands in prayer, meditation, preaching, and parish work. When the house at Schlawe was needed by the parish for other purposes, one group of ordinands moved to an empty farmstead in the more remote countryside of Gross-Schlönwitz. Although the farm did not have electricity, Dietrich arranged to have a generator installed so that he could listen to radio broadcasts. By use of coded messages and by maintaining two separate addresses where he could be reached he managed to avoid Gestapo surveillance.

After the turbulence of Berlin, Dietrich enjoyed the peace and quiet of the countryside. He wrote to his parents, "Yesterday afternoon I could not stop myself from joining the skiers in the snow-covered wood. It was really lovely, and so peaceful that everyone else seemed like a ghost."[3] One former student remembered the days of this training.

> I have a clear picture before me: the brethren [fellow students] sitting down to their afternoon coffee and their bread and jam. The chief [Dietrich] has come back after being away rather a long time . . . Now we get the latest news, and the world breaks into the peacefulness and simplicity of life on a Pomeranian estate. . . .[4]

Although church members and the pastors of the Confessing Church knew that Dietrich was still training ministers, they did not know the details, nor did they want to know. Such information was dangerous. Although the number of arrests had actually decreased, the Gestapo began to attack the Confessing Church in other ways. These measures prevented certain ministers from entering or leaving certain areas. In January 1938, Dietrich was prohibited from entering Berlin because of his church activities. His father successfully petitioned for Dietrich to be allowed to visit his family in Berlin, but he was not to go to meetings in the city. He managed to slip past the Gestapo on several occasions.

In April of 1938, Dr. Werner, chairman of the official church in Berlin and a German Christian prepared an oath for pastors as a birthday gift for Hitler. All pastors who wanted to be ordained or to remain ordained, had to swear loyalty to Hitler. A statement issued by the government indicated that Hitler didn't really care whether or not the pastors took the oath. He claimed it was an internal church affair. However, it was of importance to the German Christians, and their failure to enlist Hitler's support was a major disappointment.

Dietrich and his ordinands refused to take the oath. But as the days and months went on, more and more of the Confessing Church pastors took the oath. Dietrich felt a widening gulf between himself and the Confessing Church. While Dietrich encouraged his students and his fellow pastors to take the costly path of obedience to Christ, the German Christians wooed the "illegal pastors" with promises of steady salaries, housing, and grateful congregations. To receive such privileges they had to pledge their allegiance to Hitler and sign the Aryan Clause. With its restrictions against all those who were themselves Jewish or who had Jewish ancestors, anyone who signed the Clause not only accepted such discrimination, but gave it strength. Dietrich continued to plead with his Finkenwalde students and with other Confessing Church pastors to resist these attempts to buy their loyalty.

The night of November 9, 1938, the Nazis made war on the Jews. S.S. officers throughout the country destroyed Jewish property and took Jewish lives. Although their original orders said that the Jews themselves were not to be hindered, over one thousand were killed. According to estimates, more than 1,119 synagogues and nearly 1,000 Jewish-owned shops and stores were burned or destroyed. The night came to be called *Kristallnacht* or the Night of the Broken Glass. The next day the Nazis ordered the Jews to make all needed repairs themselves and to turn over any insurance money to the state.

Dietrich, hidden in the quiet woods of Gross-Schlönwitz with his ordinands, didn't know of the destruction until the next day. When he learned what had happened, Dietrich was outraged! He underlined a passage in his Bible in the Psalms: "they burned all the meeting places of God in the land," and wrote the date "November 9" in the margin. In a discussion with his students he said that such violence against God and humanity would not stop on its own. "If the synagogues burn today, the churches will be on fire tomorrow."[5] He waited for word from the Confessing Church that they too shared his distress, but the church was silent.

14

Dangerous Secrets

1938–1939

WHEN WORDS FAILED, it was time for action. Dietrich was spending more and more time in Berlin with his family, and when he returned to the collective pastorates, his students noticed that he seemed to be withholding information. They sensed secrets, and they were correct. Dietrich began to distance himself from the remnant of the Confessing Church and entered into active political resistance.

Almost from the beginning Dietrich had been aware of the clandestine opposition activities taking place in Germany. In the midst of total dictatorship, a few brave men and women continued to oppose Hitler. One of the most active cells of anti-Nazi conspirators existed within the Counterintelligence Office of the High Command of the Armed Forces, called the *Abwehr*. Dietrich's brother-in-law, Hans von Dohnanyi, a lawyer working within the Ministry of Justice, had given Dietrich advice and warnings that were useful to the Confessing Church. The two brothers-in-law, Dietrich and Hans, liked each other, and each recognized in the other a keen intelligence and a willingness to take action. Hans von Dohnanyi found in his brother-in-law a good listener and someone who understood his attitude toward Hitler and the Nazis. The two men met frequently in Berlin. Dohnanyi passed information to Dietrich and often asked for his advice and counsel. Eberhard Bethge noticed, as did others, that one of Dietrich's great strengths was helping others make difficult decisions. Bethge tells of a pivotal conversation between the two men.

> [Dohnanyi] asked Bonhoeffer one evening what he thought about the New Testament passage "all who take the sword will perish by the sword" (Matthew 26:52). Bonhoeffer replied that this held true for their circle [the conspirators] as well. They would have to accept that they were subject to that judgment, but there was now a need for such people who would take the responsibility for deciding its validity for themselves.[1]

Dohnanyi constantly faced life-and-death decisions, not only for himself and his family, but for all of those in the opposition and for the future of Germany. Early during Hitler's regime, Dohnanyi had come into contact with some of the leading German military officers and realized that these men shared his anxieties about the Third Reich and were prepared to take action. Dohnanyi became the pivotal figure in the political conspiracy to overthrow Hitler. During his years at the Justice Ministry, Dohnanyi began documenting what he felt were Hitler's despicable actions in what he called a "Chronicle of Shame," or more simply, his "Chronicle." When he moved to the *Abwehr* in August of 1939, he continued to add to his "Chronicle," which became longer and more incredible as Hitler's power increased. General Ludwig Beck, a member of the opposition, felt that such records could be used to explain to the world why they had plotted to take over the German government. These materials included speeches of Hitler, instructions regarding attacks on the Jewish people, background materials relating to the attacks in Poland, and lists of atrocities committed by the Nazis. More importantly, resistance leaders were hopeful that these documents would convince Germany's leading generals to turn on Hitler. The opposition circle within the *Abwehr* knew that none of the highest ranking military officers had access to the totality of Hitler's plans because each was isolated, unaware of the actions undertaken by the killing squadrons of the S.S. Those opposed to Hitler felt that they must first convince the generals to actively oppose Hitler in order to restore Germany's honor. Planning for a new Germany was an essential element of their plan, one that involved Dietrich, his brother Klaus, his brothers-in-law, and many others in the opposition.

Dohnanyi, who never joined the Nazi Party or any of its affiliates, nevertheless lived a double life as an employee of the Third Reich who was working for the overthrow of Hitler. He was not alone. Initially, those opposed to Hitler awaited Germany's defeat on the battlefield. But the German armies continued to win battle after battle.

The conspirators next tried to bring about a military coup. They approached many leading generals using the materials Dohnanyi had compiled in his "Chronicle," but the coup failed, and its failure placed Dohnanyi in an even more vulnerable, dangerous position. He moved his family to Leipzig, where he became a supreme court judge. The entire Bonhoeffer family was relieved that Hans, Christine, and their children would be in a safer position. However, Dohnanyi did not pull back on his political activities. He continued to travel to Berlin to meet with members of the resistance, including Major General Hans Oster. Admiral Wilhelm Canaris, head of Hitler's Military Intelligence Unit, the *Abwehr*, and one of the most controversial figures of the time, knew of Dohnanyi's brilliance and his determination to end Hitler's reign of terror. Canaris asked for Dohnanyi's transfer to the *Abwehr* so that Dohnanyi could worked closely with both Canaris and his chief of staff, Major General Oster.

The Bonhoeffer family home in Berlin became an important meeting place where the conspirators could exchange information. By 1938 Dietrich had been drawn deeply into conversations about a possible overthrow of the Nazi government. As Hans von Dohnanyi and Dietrich grew closer and shared their concerns and anxieties, Hans introduced Dietrich to the inner circle of conspirators. Dietrich met Canaris and Oster. Both men were respected Nazis who had become alarmed by Hitler's actions. Oster was active in the political conspiracy. Canaris provided cover while remaining at a distance from the actual planning. In fact, he continued to funnel intelligence information to Hitler while at the same time warning others of Hitler's plans of attack. Careful planning and extensive subterfuge kept the conspirators' actions from Hitler and the Gestapo, but they were constantly in danger of discovery. They selected trusted others, especially military leaders, to oppose the Nazis and to plan for a Germany without Hitler. Dietrich listened with great interest to the concerns of these intelligent and powerful men. They began to turn to him for advice and theological counsel.

Other family members were also active in the military conspiracy. Emmi Bonhoeffer, in looking back on the family's involvement in the opposition, remarked that there was no one decisive experience that drew the Bonhoeffers into action. They were certain from the beginning that Hitler was dangerous, but the increasing persecution of the Jews made it even clearer that there was no compromise with the Führer. Dietrich's brother Klaus was legal counsel for the German airline *Lufthansa*. In that position, he developed connections between various resistance groups. Some groups actively planned Hitler's overthrow; others focused on planning for life in Germany after Hitler. Rüdiger Schleicher, Dietrich's brother-in-law, was also a lawyer involved in the conspiracy. He worked with Klaus Bonhoeffer in developing plans for Germany's aviation industry after the overthrow of the Nazis. Like other members of the family, he was aware of the conspiracy and helped to hide the activities of others who were even more central to the resistance plots.

The Bonhoeffers, who had been using coded language for some time in family conversations, took even more precautions. Like other Germans opposed to Hitler's regime, they feared that the Gestapo might intercept their personal notes or phone calls and learn of their opposition. Even though foreign radio and newspapers were prohibited, Dietrich continued to listen to the radio and to read the *London Times* for as long as it was available. As the days wore on, though, he became more and more silent in church circles. He was aware of secrets that he could not share. He knew that to speak the truth now, or simply to be too outspoken, would put the lives of everyone involved in the opposition in danger.

In November 1938 all men born in 1906, including Dietrich, were required to report their place of residence to the military authorities because they would soon be called up for military service. Years earlier a young Swiss minister had asked Dietrich what he would do if called to military service under Hitler. Dietrich was silent for a long while; then he faced the young man and said, slowly but with conviction, "I hope that God in that case will give me the power not to bear arms."[2]

Now the moment had arrived and Dietrich was overwhelmed by the decision before him. If he joined the army, as required, he would have to pledge his allegiance to Hitler. Army service would inevitably require him to become a participant in the war. On the other hand, if he declared himself a pacifist, he would be forced to appear before a military tribunal and would certainly be sent to prison and possibly to his death. He was more concerned about the effect of this on the church than on himself. He wrote to his English friend and advisor George Bell, bishop of Chichester, ". . . I should cause tremendous damage to my brethren if I would make a stand on this point which would be regarded by the regime as typical of the hostility of our church toward the state."[3] His friends urged him to find a way out even if that meant leaving Germany.

In March, Dietrich left for England to visit with his sister Sabine. While there he met with Bishop Bell, who apparently reassured him about his decision to leave Germany. Dietrich stayed in England for five weeks and during that time met with a number of officials from the ecumenical movement. He told them of the state of affairs in Germany, and they assured him that the Confessing Church had much support outside of Germany.

He also met with American friends who arranged for him to travel to safety in the United States. His old friend Paul Lehmann planned for Dietrich to teach a summer course at Union Seminary, to visit and speak at other American seminaries, and to act as pastor to German immigrants in New York. While arrangement were made, Dietrich returned to Berlin, leaving again on June 2, 1939. He took a ship from England and arrived in New York on June 12. His family and friends felt that he was safe at last!

But almost from the moment he arrived in New York, Dietrich

felt uneasy. He was desperate for news from Germany, and wrote in his diary on June 28,

> . . . the newspaper reports get more and more disturbing. They distract one's thoughts. I cannot imagine that it is God's will for me to remain here without anything particular to do in case of war. I must travel at the first possible opportunity.[4]

Diary entries show him more and more anxious about the threat of war in Germany and the possibility of being marooned in the United States, unable to participate in Germany's future. His days in New York convinced him that it had been a mistake to try to escape from Germany's problems. Immediately after his decision to return to Germany, he wrote in his diary, "It [the decision to return] probably means more for me than I can see at the moment. God alone knows what. It is remarkable how I am never quite clear about the motives for any of my decisions."[5] His initial uncertainly eventually turned into a total assurance that his decision had been the right one despite the difficulties ahead. Even imprisonment and Gestapo interrogation did not make Dietrich regret his decision. Four months before his death, he was able to say to Eberhard Bethge, ". . . now I want to assure you that I haven't for a moment regretted coming back in 1939—nor any of the consequences, either. I knew quite well what I was doing, and I acted with a clear conscience."[6]

Despite strong pressure from his American friends to remain in the United States, he returned to Germany on July 8. He spent ten days with his sister in England, visited with his old friend Franz Hildebrandt, and slipped quietly back to Germany. Hellmut Traub, who had taken over Dietrich's work in the secret seminaries wrote:

> One day, after a short message that he was returning, Bonhoeffer stood before us. This was quite unexpected—indeed, there was always something extraordinary about him, even when the circumstances were quite ordinary. I was immediately up in arms, blurting out how could he come back after it had cost so much trouble to get him into safety—safety for us, for our cause; here everything was lost anyway. He very calmly lit a cigarette. Then he

said that he had made a mistake in going to America. He did not himself understand now why he had done it. His later messages from prison tell us that he never repented having returned from America.[7]

To his students Dietrich said calmly, "I know what I have chosen." To his friends in America, he wrote,

> I must live through this difficult period of our national history with the Christian people of Germany. I will have no right to participate in the reconstruction of Christian life in Germany after the war if I do not share the trials of this time with my people.[8]

The students celebrated his return with a holiday on the Baltic Coast. A message from his parents that the war was getting closer forced him to end the holiday and close the seminary. During the years when he served as director of the Confessing Church seminaries, first at Zingst and then at Finkenwalde, Dietrich had increasingly depended on others to keep the seminary functioning as he attended to the issues surrounding the church's struggle to survive.

Dietrich and Eberhard returned to the Bonhoeffers' home in Berlin for a few quiet weeks before the outbreak of war.

15

Ethics

1939–1941

ON SEPTEMBER 1, 1939, Germany invaded Poland. Without a declaration of war, Hitler sent the infantry and the air force to fight against the Polish forces, who fought stubbornly but had little chance. On September 3, 1939, Great Britain declared war on Germany. France, Australia, and New Zealand joined the declaration, but it was too late to save Poland. Warsaw surrendered on September 28.

Dietrich learned that Theodor Maass, a former student at Finkenwalde, had been killed in action at the front. Dietrich sent news of his death to all of his former Finkenwalde students via a circular letter. In the kind of comment typical of these letters, Dietrich wrote:

> . . . let us thank God in remembrance of him. He was a good brother, a quiet, faithful pastor of the Confessing church, a man who lived from word and sacrament, whom God has also thought worthy to suffer for the Gospel. . . . Where God tears great gaps we should not try to fill them with human words.[1]

Much of his time and Eberhard's was devoted to writing letters of news, comfort, and encouragement to former students in isolated parishes, prisons, or on the front lines with the German army. By

war's end, more than 80 of the 150 students who attended Finkenwalde had been killed in action.

It was also on September 1, 1939, that Hitler ordered the killing
of "incurables." A massive extermination program was organized
to eliminate the retarded and the mentally ill. Hitler had begun his
program of genetic planning in 1933 with a law that required sterilization of anyone with a genetic "weakness." Between 200,000
and 350,000 people with such conditions as deafness, mental illness, retardation, and epilepsy were forcibly sterilized. Eventually
Hitler's theories of a superior race had developed to the point
where sterilization wasn't enough. In August of 1939, a government order required doctors to register all children born with
birth defects between 1936 and 1939. The September 1 order
resulted in the death of five thousand of these children.

Charitable institutions within Germany were ordered to participate in this program by turning over to the government individuals considered mentally unfit. Typically, a family would be
notified that their son or daughter or sister had died of pneumonia or some other common illness, and that they had already been
cremated. In fact, buses manned by S.S. members picked up
selected patients at state and church institutions and drove them
to a euthanasia site, where they were killed by lethal injection or
gassed. The methods tested on these patients were later used to
kill millions of people in the death camps.

The euthanasia program was reported to the Confessing
Church leadership by pastors and directors of church institutions
for the mentally ill or disabled. The Confessing Church leaders
did not at first believe the reports and demanded more information. When word of the euthanasia program finally leaked out to
the general public, the churches protested vigorously. Many people assumed that Hitler did not know of the program because they
believed that if he were aware of it, he would stop it. They wrote
letters and held protest demonstrations. In August of 1941, after
more than seventy thousand patients and children had been
killed, Hitler publicly halted the program. In actuality, however,
the program continued throughout the war under the guise of
medical care that subjected its victims to experimental treatments

or slow starvation. Dietrich, recognizing the need for prompt action, worked with his father to obtain the medical certification needed by some pastors to keep the S.S. troops from withdrawing patients from some of the church's charitable institutions. The murder of the disabled was the beginning of the Nazi mass murder program that eventually encompassed Jews, Gypsies, and many others whom the Nazis deemed unworthy of life.

Dietrich spent increasing amounts of time with Hans von Dohnanyi and the *Abwehr* group. They turned to Dietrich for counsel and valued his opinions. They recognized that someone familiar with church and ecumenical affairs might prove useful in the future. Dietrich listened as General Beck, chief of staff of the army and a powerful member of the conspiracy, told Hans von Dohnanyi to bring his "Chronicle of Shame" up to date. Dohnanyi not only got the latest military reports, but was able to find S.S. films of the massacre of Jews in Poland. These were shown to Army generals who had indicated some degree of sympathy with a plot to rid Germany of Hitler. Everyone in the *Abwehr* group knew that in a dictatorship well-meaning citizens would not be able to bring about change without the full compliance of the leading generals. The plot to eliminate Hitler had to be, at least in part, a military coup. In addition to planning the overthrow of Hitler, the conspirators were planning for governing the new Germany.

Once the fighting on the Polish front slacked, Dietrich and Eberhard returned to the secret seminaries at Sigurdshof to continue training pastors. Dietrich left the security of the woods as often as possible to travel to Berlin. It was a hard, cold winter, and fuel to heat the buildings continued to be a problem. Dietrich made life as comfortable as possible with music and games to break up the hours of study and meditation. The last group completed their training on March 15, and, two days later, after Dietrich and Eberhard left on break, the Gestapo made it impossible to continue training pastors.

After a rest in Berlin, the Confessing Church assigned Dietrich the role of *visitator* to the churches in East Prussia. The job required him to visit various parishes, to carry information between them, to discuss theological problems with the pastors, and to serve as preacher when a pastor was called to military service. These meetings came to the notice of the Gestapo. New restrictions were imposed, and Dietrich was forbidden to speak or publish in Germany. He was required to keep the Gestapo informed about his place of residence.

Eberhard traveled with Dietrich as his assistant. On June 17, 1940, they were in a cafe in Memel when they heard the news that France had surrendered to the German Army. Everyone in the cafe jumped to their feet and began singing patriotic songs. Eberhard recalls that he and Dietrich stood up too. "Bonhoeffer raised his arm in the regulation Hitler salute, while I stood there dazed. 'Raise your arm! Are you crazy?' he whispered to me, and later: 'We shall have to run risks for very different things now, but not for that salute!'"[2]

The fall of Belgium, Holland, and France was a blow to those in the Resistance. The chance of a peaceful settlement with the English was now impossible. The fight to overthrow Hitler would be a long and difficult one for those working inside Germany. Many of the conspirators held high-profile positions within the German government and were active party members. Few people outside of Germany would have believed that any sort of resistance could survive inside the Third Reich, much less achieve success. At the beginning of the war, the German opposition hoped that Germany's failures on the battlefield would lead to Hitler's downfall, but as the German army was victorious, the possibilities for an overthrow diminished. Emmi Bonhoeffer, looking back on the era, noted:

> As long as Hitler was successful, his murder would have only led to a *Dolchstoß* ["knife in the back"] legend. People would have said, "If he hadn't been murdered, then today we would have a united Europe under German leadership." . . . This resistance was so unpopular and hard to understand; it had no echo whatsoever among the masses. I think that nowhere in the entire history of humanity has there been a resistance movement purely for moral reasons, when people are doing better from day to day.[3]

By 1940, Dietrich was actively committed to the Resistance. Canaris, Oster, and Dohnanyi enlisted him as a member of the

Abwehr. With great care and diligence, the *Abwehr* continued to function effectively as a government agency, providing Hitler with just enough information that they retained his favor, but at the same time working for Hitler's overthrow. Dietrich, as an agent of the *Abwehr*, would be freed from the burden of army service and could avoid taking the oath of allegiance that he so dreaded. He would even be relatively free of Gestapo interference. The *Abwehr* leaders decided that if asked, they could justify Dietrich's unpaid employment with the simple response that they were using Jews and communists, so they might as well use members of the Confessing Church. Over the next few years, Dietrich managed to find positions in the *Abwehr* for several of his church friends, thus saving them from military call-up or imprisonment. Eberhard Bethge, who was by this time Dietrich's closest friend and constant companion, was also employed by the *Abwehr*.

Dietrich's decision to work for the *Abwehr*, however, was not taken lightly. With that decision, he moved from the increasingly feeble Confessing Church movement into active political resistance. He put aside pacifist notions and, like Dohnanyi, took up the sword and was prepared to pay with his life, if necessary. What made Dietrich, the pacifist, take such a radical step into active political opposition? In a Christmas letter to Hans von Dohnanyi and friends in the conspiracy, written in 1942, Dietrich explained his motivation for political action:

> We are not Christ, but if we want to be Christians, we must have some share in Christ's largeheartedness by acting with responsibility and in freedom when the hour of danger comes, and by showing a real compassion that springs, not from fear, but from the liberating and redeeming love of Christ for all who suffer. Mere waiting and looking on is not Christian behavior. Christians are called to compassion and action, not in the first place by their own sufferings, but by the sufferings of their brothers and sisters, for whose sake Christ suffered.[4]

He vowed to continue working for a "better future" until the day of judgment, but the life of deception did not come naturally to Dietrich. The former outspoken pastor was now quiet, and it appeared to others, former friends and colleagues familiar with the church struggles, that he had rejected the Confessing Church, biblical teachings, and his own arguments against the Nazis. As Dietrich wrote to his family and fellow conspirators in his Christmas letter,

> We have been silent witnesses of evil deeds; we have been drenched by many storms; we have learnt the arts of equivocation and pretense; experience has made us suspicious of others and kept us from being truthful and open; intolerable conflicts have worn us down and even made us cynical.[5]

Because he could not share his secret life as a conspirator with his colleagues or friends, they assumed that he was giving away church secrets to Hitler's government. If he denied their suspicions, he risked revealing the extent to which the *Abwehr* itself was involved in the attempt to overthrow Hitler. To Confessing Church colleagues he appeared to be a traitor to their cause, but church officials beyond Germany's borders eventually realized that he was trying to save Germany's people—Jewish and Christian—from Nazi terrorism. Dietrich himself had long ceased to care what others thought of him, and he had become cynical about the possibility of receiving significant assistance from the Confessing Church. In a letter to Eberhard Bethge in 1967, Karl Barth admitted:

> It was new to me above all else that Bonhoeffer was the first, yes, indeed almost the only, theologian who in the years after 1933 concentrated energetically on the question of the Jews and dealt with it energetically. For a long time now I have considered myself guilty of not having raised it with equal emphasis during the church struggle. . . .[6]

Dietrich's sister-in-law, Emmi Bonhoeffer, noted that it was the increased persecution against the Jews that Dietrich witnessed on his return from America that convinced him that he must make the move into active political resistance. He was now prepared to take whatever action was required to stop the madness. As Eberhard Bethge wrote,

> In giving himself over to the logic of the conspiracy, he had to allow himself to be exploited as a man of the Church and of ecumenism. He could be made use of as an ecumenically known pastor who, by

being trusted in Allied circles, made new contacts which were urgently needed by the conspiracy. He could not expect the leaders of the conspiracy to grant him special treatment because he was a clergyman. He had to share totally in camouflage and deceit.[7]

Dietrich wrote reports on the ecumenical movement for the *Abwehr*, but these reports didn't provide any significant information to the Nazis. They did, however, provide a convincing front for the claim that his work was supporting Hitler's war efforts. His resistance work required him to travel throughout Europe trying to convince church officials to support the Resistance fighters in their plot to overthrow Hitler. Dietrich's success depended on his ability to convince church leaders of the truth of his claims. These church officials, in turn, would try to convince the political leaders of their countries that the German Resistance was at work and in need of assistance. The Resistance planned for a future after Hitler and wanted the support of the Allies in rebuilding a new Germany.

When not needed to carry messages for the Resistance, Dietrich continued his theological work at his parents' home at Marienburger Allee 43 in Berlin. Eberhard often stayed with the Bonhoeffers too, even though he had his own apartment in town. He was accepted as a member of the family and joined in family musical evenings as flute player.

Dietrich had begun work on another book, *Ethics*, which he never completed. The two men debated and discussed theological issues, and Eberhard helped Dietrich to focus and refine his thinking. Two years later when he was working on the project in his prison cell, he wrote to Eberhard, "I sometimes feel as if my life were more or less over, and as if all I had to do now were to finish my *Ethics*."[8]

Dietrich never had the chance to complete his work or to add the finishing touches. It was Eberhard Bethge who eventually pieced the fragments together into a book published in 1949. Their long hours of discussion and the letters the men exchanged while Dietrich was in prison contributed greatly to the finished manuscript. In *Ethics*, Dietrich spoke directly to the ethical dilemmas posed by the war and by Nazi treatment of the Jews; he explored the relationship of the church to the world and the role of the Christian to the church, the world, and to Jesus Christ. He says that ". . . Jesus Christ was the promised Messiah of the Israelite-Jewish people, and for that reason the line of our forefathers goes back beyond the appearance of Jesus Christ to the people of Israel. Western history is, by God's will, indissolubly linked with the people of Israel. . . . "[9] The persecution of the Jews and the silence of the church informed his thinking. He did not hesitate to speak of the guilt of a church that participates in oppression, hatred, and even murder of the weakest members of the society. He called Christians back to the gospel, the confessions, and the teachings of Jesus Christ. In his prison letters to Eberhard Bethge he further defined his thinking about Christian responsibility and God's place in the world. In a letter dated July 21, 1944, the day after a failed attempt to assassinate Hitler, Dietrich wrote to Eberhard "that it is only by living completely in this world that one learns to have faith." By the time he wrote these words, Dietrich had become active in the political resistance and had worked to bring about Hitler's overthrow. He knew that this failed assassination attempt could result in his own death sentence if the extent of his involvement became known. He went on to say:

> I mean living unreservedly in life's duties, problems, successes and failures, experiences and perplexities. In so doing we throw ourselves completely into the arms of God, taking seriously, not our own sufferings, but those of God in the world—watching with Christ in Gethsemane.[10]

In September and October he returned to the country estate of Ruth von Kleist-Retzow, where he used the quiet time to work. From November 1940 until February 1941 he moved to the monastery in Ettal, where he continued his writing and awaited further assignments from the *Abwehr*. A Catholic friend in the Resistance, Dr. Joseph Müller, arranged for Dietrich to meet the abbot and to take up residence in the monastery. Dietrich felt quite at home among the Catholic brothers. It was an atmosphere that reminded him of the happy days in the community house at Finkenwalde.

16

Deceptions for Peace

1941–1943

I N FEBRUARY 1941 Dietrich was assigned to the *Abwehr* office in Munich. While in Munich he stayed with his aunt, Countess Christine Klackreuth. On February 24 he left for Switzerland on an assignment for the *Abwehr*. General Oster and Hans von Dohnanyi hoped that Dietrich would have credibility among ecumenical leaders. He was expected to establish connections with the foreign churches and to convince them that Resistance activities were taking place in Germany. If they showed interest, he anticipated exploring ideas about a possible peace with Germany after Hitler's defeat.

The trip had been delayed for several weeks while he gathered foreign currency and a proper passport. When he finally reached the Swiss border, he was required to provide the name of a Swiss citizen who would vouch for him. Karl Barth was the obvious choice. Barth gave permission hesitantly, wondering whether Dietrich Bonhoeffer had turned into a Hitler supporter. How could a Confessing Church pastor get the proper papers for traveling in the midst of war? The two men met during Dietrich's travels in Switzerland, and Dietrich then explained fully his involvement with the opposition.

Dietrich stayed in Switzerland for four weeks and took the

opportunity to visit his friend Erwin Sutz and to send letters to his sister Sabine and to Bishop Bell in England. It was a great joy for Dietrich to be able to write to Sabine. Once war had broken out, the exchange of letters between Germany and England had become impossible.

Dietrich met with a number of important church leaders in Geneva. When he suggested that there was a resistance organization in Germany, few believed him. Willem Visser 't Hooft, a prominent Dutch ecumenical leader who served as the secretary-general of the World Council of Churches, listened intently. After the visit, Visser 't Hooft wrote to Bishop Bell, "Bonhoeffer was a week with us and spent most of his time extracting ecumenical information from persons and documents. . . . we learned a lot from him."[1] Dietrich had managed to convince important people in the ecumenical movement that the Resistance was working hard despite the problems in Germany. What they needed, Dietrich explained, was a signal from the Allies that once the Nazis were overthrown, the Allies were prepared to recognize a new German government. Would the Allied governments support the conspirators? Dietrich left with his reputation restored and the door open for several more visits to Switzerland.

Although most of his time was spent in serious discussion about church and political matters, he did find time for pleasure. Adolf Freudenberg, with whom Dietrich stayed in Geneva, tells of the time that Dietrich visited in 1942. Freudenberg's wife, noting the shabby nature of Dietrich's clothes, took him shopping. When she returned, she exclaimed: "I have never had such a joyful and grateful customer. Bonhoeffer tried on the new underpants and looked at them blissfully, and only regretted that he could not walk along the street in them so that people might see their beauty."[2] Dietrich's charm won over many people. He seemed to have an unusual ability to find joy and beauty in everyday situations.

Dietrich stayed in touch with the Confessing Church leadership, but he did so carefully because of the restrictions that the Nazis had placed on his church involvement. He had been prohibited from speaking; now he was prohibited from publishing.

The prohibition included theological works. Nevertheless, Dietrich helped several members of the clergy avoid military service by getting them deferments through his contacts in the *Abwehr*. Despite his efforts and those of his brother-in-law, many of the young illegal pastors were conscripted for active military duty. Dietrich himself managed to avoid the draft only because Dohnanyi and Oster declared him officially indispensable. This attempt to avoid military service and to help those in the Confessing Church to do likewise was included in the charges against both Dietrich and Hans von Dohnanyi during their trials in 1944.

Dietrich was almost constantly on the move. He returned from Switzerland to the country home in Friedrichsbrunn, then commuted between Klein-Krössin, Berlin, and Munich. The news from Berlin was ominous. On September 1, 1941, Hitler issued a decree that all Jews over the age of six must wear a yellow star. By mid-October, deportations had begun. Jewish citizens were herded together and taken away to concentration camps. Dietrich and his friend Justus Perels wrote a report on the deportations that they turned over to Dohnanyi and Oster. A few pastors spoke out boldly on behalf of the Jews. Katharina Staritz, a woman pastor in Breslau, published an article defending the Jews and was immediately arrested. A few church members helped Jews to obtain illegal papers and to vanish, but in the face of such overwhelming odds, most people remained silent.

Dietrich himself said little in public, but plunged into a bold plan to help a few Jews escape to Switzerland. The plan, called Operation 7, was designed by the *Abwehr* to help save seven Jews who were known by the conspirators. As time passed, the number increased to fourteen. The operation took over a year to complete. First, the Jews had to be freed from the deportation lists. Dohnanyi worked tirelessly to obtain safe-conduct passes for them. Then they were made agents of the *Abwehr*. Once they were agents they would be able to leave Germany, but getting them into Switzerland proved difficult. The Swiss intended to remain neutral. They would not accept German Jews. Dietrich, Perels, and Wilhelm Rott, who had worked with Dietrich at Finkenwalde, appealed to Swiss church officials. Finally, permission was granted. Even then, arrangements were not complete until Dohnanyi deposited foreign money into a Swiss account to support the Operation 7 group.

The first to go was Charlotte Friedenthal, a woman who had worked closely with Dietrich's friend Wilhelm Rott in the provisional government of the Confessing Church. She arrived in Basle, Switzerland, safely after a hectic journey. Her arrival proved that the others could also make the escape. A month later, the rest of the group followed. Although the operation seemed to go smoothly, the Gestapo was suspicious. They investigated, but did not discover any irregularities. Later, however, Operation 7 became a major part of the evidence used to arrest Dietrich, his sister Christine von Dohnanyi, and her husband.

Dietrich spent October and November of 1941 at his parents' home in Berlin recovering from pneumonia. He had already moved most of his books from the secret seminaries to his attic room, and he even found room for a clavichord which he had purchased in 1938. He was also spending time in a remote mountain monastery in Ettal working on *Ethics*.

Nazi action against the Jews was increasing. On January 20, 1942, the Wannsee Conference was held at an estate in Berlin. The conference between party officers and the S.S. established the procedures to be used in creating a "Final Solution to the Jewish Question." According to figures presented at this conference, 537,000 Jews had emigrated. The remaining Jews would be sent to death camps, where they would be murdered. Many had already died in concentration campus. By 1943 another 143,000 Jews had been killed in the gas chambers. The Jews who participated in Operation 7 had escaped Germany only a few months before.

In April of 1942, Dietrich and Helmuth von Moltke, another *Abwehr* agent, went to Norway to meet with church leaders to encourage them to continue their efforts at resistance. Nazi invasion in Norway at first led to severe restrictions against the pastors. The Norwegian pastors, however, showed great courage in the face of Nazi oppression. All the bishops refused to perform official functions and remained on the job only as pastors to the people. The Catholic clergy did the same. When the Nazis tried to establish a Hitler Youth program in Norway, a thousand teachers resigned. Pastors, priests, and teachers were on strike. The very plan that Dietrich had proposed to the German pastors in 1933 worked in Norway in 1942. The *Abwehr* helped to convince leaders in Germany that a more general people's revolt would follow in Norway unless the German government pulled back. Such logic was obvious. The Nazis relented and gave back some of the religious and educational freedoms that they had taken from the Norwegians.

Dietrich was aware of many of the German resistance groups. The White Rose, a student group organized by Hans Scholl, Sophie Scholl, and Christoph Probst in Munich, was also aware of Dietrich Bonhoeffer. They planned a secret meeting with Dietrich, but because of the time needed to set up such meetings, it was delayed. Sadly, the White Rose organization was discovered by the Nazis, and the student leaders were tried and executed before the meeting could take place. Helmuth von Moltke, with whom Dietrich had ample time for conversation during the trip to Norway, was the founder of a resistance group known as the Kreisau Circle. Moltke and his group did not desire the violent removal of Hitler, but sought to bring about dissolution of the Third Reich through other means. Dietrich had come to believe that only Hitler's death would end the horrors. He recognized that his ability to serve the church in the future was already compromised, but that Hitler's assassination was necessary, he did not doubt.

Dietrich's next trip was to Sweden to meet with Bishop Bell and to secure British support for the Resistance movement. Long talks with Bishop Bell convinced the influential churchman that the German Resistance was well organized and was prepared to take action. As Bell later wrote,

> When Bonhoeffer and I were alone I asked him very privately if he could tell me the names of the chief conspirators. He gave them at once. . . . I could see that as he told me these facts he was full of sorrow that things had come to such a pass in Germany and that action like this was necessary.[3]

Dietrich explained that a word of support from the British would have a profound effect on the Resistance leaders. All their carefully laid plans depended on British assurance that after the Nazis were defeated, the Germans would be given another chance to establish their own government. Bell promised to help, but despite extensive efforts he failed to convince important British officials to send an encouraging word to the *Abwehr* group. Visser 't Hooft reported that his own efforts also met with failure. Both later lamented the shortsightedness of their governments. Dietrich and his friends waited in vain for a response. Meanwhile, they continued with plans to assassinate Hitler.

On a personal level, Dietrich was strengthened by his meetings with Bishop Bell. He wrote to Bell:

> . . . this spirit of fellowship and of Christian brotherliness will carry me through the darkest hour, and even if things go worse than we hope and expect, the light of these few days will never extinguish in my heart. . . . Please pray for us.[4]

Dietrich's next trip was to Italy with Hans von Dohnanyi, where they met with members of the Italian Resistance to explore the possibility of the groups working together. When Dietrich returned to Germany, there was no *Abwehr* assignment awaiting him. He took the opportunity to spend some time in the Pomeranian countryside with Ruth von Kleist-Restow. He'd been there briefly between his trips to Sweden and Italy and had chanced to meet Maria von Wedemeyer. Maria, a granddaughter of Ruth von Kleist-Retzow, was eighteen. Dietrich was twice her age. For years he had put aside the idea of marriage in such troubled times, but something about Maria so appealed to him that he returned after the trip to Italy to visit with her again. Maria was bright, lively, and had an inventive mind. She was also beautiful. The more time they spent together, the deeper they came to love each other. They managed to meet in Berlin and also at Maria's grandmother's home in Klein-Kossin.

It had been a difficult year for Maria's family. Her father had been killed on the Eastern Front, and her brothers and cousins were serving on other front lines. When Dietrich asked for permission to marry Maria, her mother hesitated. She was worried about the age difference and about Dietrich's dangerous work. She asked that the couple wait a year to become engaged and that they not see each other during that time. Dietrich refused. How could he abide by such rules? Eventually Frau von Wedemeyer relented and Dietrich and Maria were engaged on January 17, 1943. At a time of extreme danger, at a time when the world around them was collapsing, Dietrich and Maria enjoyed planning for a future together in a world at peace.

17

Arrest

1943

ALL OF THE CONSPIRATORS in the *Abwehr* were fully aware of the existence of the death camps. They knew that the horrors would not end until Hitler was dead. Months of careful planning and preparation led to the first attempt on Hitler's life. On March 7, 1943, General Oster, Admiral Canaris, and Hans von Dohnanyi traveled to Smolensk carrying a box of explosives. They were supposedly holding a general intelligence meeting, but in actuality were making the final arrangements for an assassination attempt.

Lieutenant Fabian von Schlabrendorff and General Henning von Tresckow managed to get the time bomb onto Hitler's plane. The bomb, disguised as a gift of two bottles of brandy, was set to explode thirty minutes after take-off. It should have exploded after about 125 to 150 miles of flight. But the explosion never occurred. Something went wrong with the bomb.

Schlabrendorff raced to East Prussia to retrieve the bomb before it was discovered. Fortunately, the assassination attempt was not detected by Hitler or those charged with his protection. The bomb was transported back to the *Abwehr*, where it was taken apart, and the conspirators discovered that it was probably the excessive cold in the plane's cargo hold that prevented the bomb from exploding.

Dietrich, Eberhard, and the Bonhoeffer family waited anxiously for news of the assassination. It was difficult to hide their disappointment on hearing that the plot had failed. More secret meetings and more planning convinced the conspirators to make another attempt on March 16 at a ceremony that Hitler planned to attend. This time Colonel von Gersdorff agreed to carry the bomb into Hitler's very presence. If necessary, he was prepared to blow himself up in the process of killing Hitler.

As Hitler toured an army museum, Gersdorff was to show Hitler an exhibit of captured war materials. Gersdorff and the conspirators worked tirelessly to prepare for the attempt, but as the date drew closer, they met all sorts of obstacles. First, Hitler postponed the ceremony until March 21. Then the conspirators had trouble finding a fuse that would set off the bomb without a long delay. Finally, Gersdorff had to get close to Hitler without alarming Hitler's body guards, and he had to light the bomb's fuse at just the right time without drawing any attention to his actions.

While Gersdorff awaited Hitler's appearance at the ceremony, Dietrich and his family were all together in the Bonhoeffer home in Berlin. They had gathered for Karl Bonhoeffer's seventy-fifth birthday and were planning to perform a musical cantata as a part of the celebration. The children focused on the musical, but Dietrich and Hans anxiously waited for the phone to ring with news of the assassination. Hans von Dohnanyi had his car ready and waiting so that he could rush to the new government headquarters. But the phone never rang. This attempt, too, failed. Gersdorff had expected Hitler to linger over the war exhibit, but Hitler rushed through the museum, barely stopping anywhere. Gersdorff lit one fuse, but could not light the other without drawing attention to himself. He still felt confident that the bomb would go off during the time that Hitler examined the museum exhibit next to Gersdorff. Hitler left the building before the bomb detonated. Gersdorff was able to defuse the bomb in a nearby restroom, and the only consolation for the conspirators was that this plot also went undiscovered. They were determined to try again. By the time of the third attempt, however, Dietrich and Hans von Dohnanyi had been in prison for over a year.

For years Dietrich had been defying Hitler in one way or another, and his actions had not escaped the notice of the Gestapo. In 1936 he had been forbidden to teach, in 1940 to preach, and in 1941 to publish. His travel was restricted, his seminary closed. He had spoken openly in opposition to Hitler despite the danger, had trained pastors illegally, and apparently without the knowledge of the Gestapo he had helped fourteen Jews to emigrate in the plan called Operation 7. He knew the details of each planned assassination attempt; he supported and encouraged the conspirators. As far as he knew the Gestapo was not aware of his negotiations with foreign nations or his involvement with the plot to kill Hitler. Nevertheless, he knew that his arrest could occur any day.

In analyzing the German resistance, Robert Weldon Whalen concluded that the participants in the Resistance had several things in common. Most were men and many of them were related; they were brothers, in-laws, and cousins. They were Christians; they were, by and large, professionally trained and held prominent positions. They came from wealthy, often aristocratic, families. They believed in self-sacrifice, and, Whalen concludes,

> the conspirators were persons of hope, not optimism. They had few illusions about human nature, they had little confidence that history would automatically improve, they knew full well the capacity of human beings for evil.[1]

In his 1942 Christmas letter to his family and members of the conspiracy Dietrich said, "It may be that the day of judgment will dawn tomorrow; in that case, we shall gladly stop working for a better future. But not before. . . . We still love life, but I do not think that death can take us by surprise now."[2] The conspirators continued to plan for a better Germany, one without Hitler, because it had become their duty, no matter the self-sacrifice it might require.

On April 5, 1943, Dietrich called his sister Christine. An unknown man answered the phone. Dietrich guessed that Hans

and Christine had been arrested and that the Gestapo were searching the house. Dietrich checked his room. He had already hidden
any incriminating papers in the ceiling and everything seemed to
be in order. Calmly he and Eberhard walked next door to his sister Ursula's home. She prepared him a good meal. He ate. And
then he waited, supported by Ursula and Eberhard, knowing
what might lay ahead, fearing what might lay ahead, but certain
that the path of active resistance to Hitler had been the right
choice, no matter the consequences. Dietrich had thought often
about the possibility of going to prison. In 1937 he had written his
brother Karl-Friedrich, "Certainly none of us is eager to go to
prison. However, if it does come to that, then we shall do so—
hopefully, anyway—with joy since it is such a worthy cause."[3]

It was four o'clock when Dietrich's father walked next door to
tell Dietrich that there were two men waiting to see him in his
room. Dietrich returned home where the men waited. They had
neither an arrest warrant nor a search warrant, but they searched
his room and finally ordered Dietrich to their car. He walked from
the house with his Bible in his hands. He parents, his sister, and
his faithful friend Eberhard Bethge watched as he got into the
Gestapo car for the short trip to Tegel Prison. They never saw him
outside of the prison gates again.

The reception cell at Tegel Prison was cold, but Dietrich could
not bear to touch the greasy, stinking blankets on his cot. He heard
crying from the cell next door. No one came to investigate. He
slept fitfully, if at all, that first night in prison and awoke when
someone tossed a slice of dry bread into his cell. Later that day he
was moved to an area reserved for those condemned to death. A
few days later the interrogations began.

Dietrich had visited enough of his former students in prison to
be aware of how harsh a life behind bars could be. He spent the
first twelve days in solitary confinement in the topmost cell in
Tegel. After forty-eight hours his Bible was returned to him, but he
was forbidden newspapers, cigarettes, or exercise in the prison
courtyard. On his cell hung a sign prohibiting anyone from speaking to him. During those lonely days, Dietrich considered suicide.
"Suicide," he scribbled on a scrap of paper, "not from a sense of

guilt, but because basically I am already dead."[4] He wondered if perhaps he had caused his friends and family great grief out of mistaken motives. Doubts assailed him during those dreary first days. His prison cell, which was about six feet by nine feet and furnished only with a bed, a shelf, a stool, and a bucket, did not even allow him to see outside. The only window was a skylight in the wall above the bed, and it was so high that there was no way Dietrich could see outside. Eventually he would be allowed to walk in the prison yard and to receive food packages from his family.

In the 1942 essay, "After Ten Years," Dietrich wrote, "Fundamentally we feel that we really belong to death already, and that every new day is a miracle."[5] After the first disheartening days in jail, and with his Bible as his guide, Dietrich began to look at every new day as a miracle. He worried, of course, about Hans von Dohnanyi and his sister Christine, but put his faith in God. Eventually, his fellow prisoners would describe him as "radiating so much peace"and "always cheerful" despite the suffering imposed by prison life.[6]

His first letter from prison was a short reassuring note to his parents, "I do want you to be quite sure that I am all right."[7] He wrote that he was getting plenty of sleep and was finding comfort in remembering the hymns of Paul Gerhardt, his favorite composer. He had a Bible and some writing paper. The letter, like all those to his parents, was carefully designed to relieve their concerns. He spoke of his joy at hearing a thrush in the prison garden "which sings a beautiful little song every morning, and now he has started in the evening, too. One is grateful for little things. . . ."[8]

18

Letters from Prison

1943–1944

DIETRICH QUICKLY ADAPTED the routine of Finkenwalde to life in a prison cell. He woke early, meditated, prayed, and tried to continue his writing. He took exercise, either in his small cell or, when allowed, in the prison yard. Harald Poelchau, who served as prison chaplain in Tegel Prison while Dietrich was a prisoner recalled that "during air raids, and during the exercises in the yard, Bonhoeffer became the pastor of his fellow prisoners, and even, increasingly, of his warders."[1]

Dietrich was interrogated, and like most Gestapo prisoners, he feared that he would reveal secrets that could lead to the arrest of other conspirators. He told another prisoner that the interrogators had threatened to apply torture and that they were brutal when questioning him. He managed to play the wrongly accused pastor throughout the interrogations exactly as he and Dohnanyi had planned. If Dietrich did not play his part well or stick to the agreed-upon story, his testimony would endanger the Dohnanyis. After each session with the interrogators, Dietrich wrote a detailed response to try to clear up any errors in his testimony lest others suffer for his mistakes.

The charges against Dietrich, although not stated specifically at first, were that he committed "high treason and treason against one's country."[2] He was questioned on four main topics: his attempt to avoid Gestapo surveillance by joining the *Abwehr*, his role in Operation 7, his journeys outside Germany to meet church officials, and his role in arranging for a number of Confessing Church pastors to avoid military service. Hans von Dohnanyi was questioned on the same topics. For a long time, the Gestapo remained unaware of the extent of Dietrich's involvement in the conspiracy to assassinate Hitler.

His family was also able to make his prison life easier by asking Dietrich's uncle, General Paul von Hase, the military commandant of Berlin, to visit Dietrich in prison. This impressed the prison commander, who allowed Dietrich small privileges and made sure he received his weekly packages. Dietrich was somewhat embarrassed by the special treatment he received, but used his influence whenever possible to help other inmates. Dietrich's parents sent him food, which helped him to keep up his strength, clean clothes and tobacco, which helped keep up his spirits, and books, which helped him to continue writing his *Ethics*. Dietrich spent several hours in his cell each day reading and studying theology.

Secret messages were often included in the family's packages. Because all parcels and letters were searched by censors, the messages were cleverly concealed. The Bonhoeffer family had planned well in advance for the eventual imprisonment of those involved in the conspiracy. One method those on the outside used to send messages involved making marks on the pages of the books that Dietrich requested from his family. As Eberhard Bethge describes it, "If the owner's name, 'D. Bonhoeffer,' was underlined in the book, that meant that it contained a message. The message was entered by putting a faint pencil mark under a letter every ten pages, starting from the back."[3] The letters made up sentences which informed Dietrich about the progress with the conspiracy or the nature of the testimony given by others to the Gestapo. He could then provide information that matched what the Gestapo already knew. He sent messages to his family in the same fashion when he returned the books to them. The Bonhoeffers spent hours working out these messages in order to help Dietrich and the other men in prison.

Dietrich befriended prisoners and guards alike. Those in the infirmary often called him down to help in the evenings, and he spent hours in conversation with them or even listening to the radio. Certain guards occasionally allowed him unsupervised visits with his family or with Eberhard Bethge or even with Maria. Dietrich's younger sister, Susanne, wrote of a visit engineered by a friendly guard. She traveled to Tegel by bicycle. On her return home, she wrote about the event. "My turn has come to hand in what I have brought for Dietrich. Strict examination. Nobody ever notices the dots under the letters in the books which we bring and fetch, our code." She received an exchange parcel from Dietrich— laundry, empty containers, books he has finished. And then . . .

> I am just packing everything into my shabby little suitcase when one of the uniformed men beckons to me saying: "You wanted to make a telephone call." Later I hear that this is Sergeant Holzendorf. Of course, why shouldn't I? He may want to give me a message. I walk behind him, through narrow grayish corridors. Not a word. Then he opens a door, says "fifteen minutes," steps back, and closes the door behind me. I see my brother before me.[4]

Susanne and Dietrich made use of the unexpected gift of a visit to exchange vital information about other family members who were in jail, about interrogations, about plans for the trials. The guard, Sergeant Holzendorf, was not the only one to give Dietrich such favors as a way of returning the time and attention that Dietrich gave to the guards. Even Harald Poelchau, the chaplain, noticed that

> Toward the end of June 1944 he [Dietrich] moved so freely about the house [prison] that we seriously wondered whether he should not escape, which could have been easily arranged. He did not want to do it; it would have meant inflicting himself on somebody who had to hide him.[5]

In a poem written in June of 1944, Dietrich himself comments on his prison existence.

> Who Am I? They often tell me I would step from my prison
> cell poised, cheerful and sturdy,
> like a nobleman from his country estate.
> Who am I? They often tell me I would speak with my guards
> freely, pleasantly and firmly,
> as if I had it to command.[6]

He goes on to say that what others may tell him is not what he feels about himself. He is "restless, yearning, sick, like a bird in its cage. . . ." His poem describes his anguish at being confined, his anger at the "tyranny" he sees in the prison, and his worry for "friends far away." The poem ends with a stirring statement. "Whoever I am, you know me, O God. You know I am yours."

Faith made each day bearable. The Bible provided support, and recollected hymns provided comfort. And it was books and letters that helped Dietrich focus his thinking, both personal and intellectual, during the trying days of imprisonment. The first letters were stilted, subject to censorship, and designed to reassure family that he was well. Gradually, as weeks passed and Dietrich befriended certain guards, he was able to avoid the censors and his letters became vibrant, reflecting his own situation and his hopes for the future. Because the letters were smuggled out of prison by the guards, and so escaped the censors, Dietrich and Eberhard were able to speak freely in matters both personal and theological. In the letters to Eberhard, Dietrich revisited many of the theological concerns of their earlier discussions. Christian activity must not be restricted to the church, he wrote, but the Christian must see God at the center of life. When writing to Eberhard, Dietrich could clarify his theological concerns, knowing that his thoughtful friend would read carefully and respond helpfully. "What is bothering me incessantly," Dietrich wrote, "is the question what Christianity really is, or indeed who Christ really is, for us today."[7]

Through prayer, Bible reading, and his correspondence with Eberhard, Dietrich arrived at provocative answers. He wrote:

> It always seems to me that we are trying anxiously in this way to
> reserve some space for God; I should like to speak of God not on

the boundaries but at the centre, not in weaknesses but in strength; and therefore not in death and guilt but in man's life and goodness.[8]

The ideas that Dietrich discussed with Eberhard in his letters continue to provoke theological debate and discussion. In his letter of July 8, 1944, he wrote to Eberhard:

By the way, it would be very nice if you didn't throw away my theological letters. . . . One writes some things more freely and more vividly in a letter than in a book, and often I have better thoughts in a conversation by correspondence than by myself.[9]

Eberhard did manage to save most of the letters, although some were lost due to the conditions of war.

About a month after Dietrich was imprisoned, Eberhard Bethge married Renate Schleicher, Dietrich's niece. Eberhard, who had become like a member of the Bonhoeffer family, now was family through this marriage. Over the years when Dietrich and Eberhard had returned to the Bonhoeffer home, Eberhard gradually fell in love with the oldest daughter of Ursula and Rüdiger Schleicher, Renate, who lived in the house next door. In 1943 she was only sixteen, and Eberhard was nearly twenty years her senior. Although her parents were reluctant at first to have her marry at so young an age, they relented, not only because they liked Eberhard, but because Renate would soon be called up for military service. It was one of the few ways available to avoid the draft. The couple was more than willing to wait to marry until Dietrich was released from prison, but he urged them to go ahead. He was certainly aware of the crisis facing Renate and of the uncertainty over his own case.

From his prison cell, Dietrich wrote a sermon for the occasion, and one of the guards delivered it to the Bonhoeffer home for him. In that sermon, he told the couple,

In a word, live together in the forgiveness of your sins, for without it no human fellowship, least of all a marriage, can survive. Don't insist on your rights, don't blame each other, don't judge or condemn each other, don't find fault with each other, but accept each other as you are, and forgive each other every day from the bottom of your hearts.[10]

For Dietrich, alone in his prison cell, the wedding must have been a painful reminder of his separation from Maria. Eventually Maria was allowed to send letters and even to visit Dietrich, but the separation was terribly difficult for them both. Many of Dietrich's letters to Maria discuss the details of their wedding and their life together. Dietrich enjoyed imagining how they would decorate their home, raise their children, spend their days together. These homey distractions gave the couple a bit of normalcy in the midst of an abnormal and unbearable situation. Despite his efforts to remain hopeful, the time in prison was agonizing. In a letter to Eberhard, he wrote about the situation: "We have been engaged now for nearly a year and have never been alone together for one hour! Isn't it absurd. . . ."[11]

Dietrich had introduced Maria to his family years before as the granddaughter of his friend from Finkenwalde, Ruth von Kleist-Retzow. Dietrich's nieces and nephews had spent time at the Kleist-Retzow estate during the summers, and some of Ruth von Kleist-Retzow's grandchildren had visited the Bonhoeffers in Berlin. After Dietrich was imprisoned, Maria spent time with the Bonhoeffers in Berlin. This was not only helpful to his parents but a great comfort to Dietrich. His family and friends continued to hope for his eventual release and focused their efforts on the trial.

Thanks to coded messages from family both Dietrich and Hans von Dohnanyi knew that another assassination attempt was planned for July 1944. If it succeeded, the charges would be dropped. Hans took extreme measures to delay his trial until after the planned assassination. During the summer of 1943, he developed a serious illness. In November, when Allied bombing raids destroyed the part of the prison where Dohnanyi was held, he was injured and suffered a brain embolism. He spent several months under medical care in a hospital. Another time he ingested live diphtheria bacteria so that his illness would delay the trial. Delay was essential, he felt, to give the conspirators time to bring their final plans to pass.

On July 20, 1944, the final assassination attempt was made.

Count Claus Schenk von Stauffenberg, an army colonel, carried an explosive into a meeting with Hitler at Wolfschanze, about three hundred miles from Berlin. Stauffenberg managed to place his briefcase near Hitler, and then excused himself to make a phone call. Stauffenberg hurried into a waiting car and headed to the airfield. The bomb exploded at 12:50 P.M. Everyone in the room was bruised or burned by the explosion. Four were killed. But not Hitler. He was cut and bruised and his eardrums were pierced, but he was able to continue with planned activities almost as if nothing had happened. Hitler immediately ordered all those associated with the July 20 plot found and tried. About two hundred people involved in the plot, including Stauffenberg, were located and tried by the "People's Court." Their deaths followed immediately. Some of those involved committed suicide. Some estimates indicate that by the end of the war over seven thousand people were arrested in connection with the assassination plot. There is no evidence that more than a few hundred were actually involved. Families of those arrested were often sent to concentration camps and children were sent to live in Nazi-approved foster homes.

Dietrich and the other conspirators in prison were aware of the preparations for Stauffenberg's assassination plan. How anxiously the prisoners must have waited for the word that Hitler was dead and that Germany was freed from Nazi domination. Dietrich heard the news of the failed attempt on the radio in the prison infirmary. His letter to Eberhard immediately after the failed assassination attempt expressed his abiding faith in God and his belief that "it is only by living completely in this world that one learns to believe." He concluded with the prayer, "May God in his mercy lead us through these times. But above all may he lead us to himself!"[12]

The Bonhoeffer family prayed that Dietrich and Hans would not be connected to the plot. After all, they had been in prison when the assassination attempt occurred. For a long time, nothing happened to change their situation and the family dared to feel some relief from their constant anxiety. Dietrich continued his Bible study, reading, and writing.

Eberhard Bethge also waited for news. Like Dietrich, he had been recruited to work for the *Abwehr*. After Dietrich's arrest, Eberhard was drafted into the German army. Thanks to his *Abwehr* connections, however, he was sent to an intelligence unit in northern Italy, where he worked as a clerk. He heard on the radio in Italy that an attempt to assassinate Hitler had failed. His first reaction was, "If the dispatches were even close to accurate, was everything lost for the family, for the prisoners, and for a different Germany?"[13] Eberhard did not know the fate of his family and friends for days.

First came a letter from his wife, Renate, but she had no news of the family in prison. Finally Eberhard received several letters from Dietrich. These included the poem "Who Am I," which Eberhard copied immediately and gave to an officer on his way back to Berlin. Eberhard was amazed that the letters from prison continued to arrive at his army outpost. The correspondence, which continued thanks to the kind prison guard Corporal Knobloch, allowed Dietrich to send coded advice to Eberhard in case he too was arrested for his involvement with the *Abwehr*'s various operations.

In August of 1944 the situation for Dietrich and his family worsened. The Gestapo discovered Hans von Dohnanyi's "Chronicle," which listed in great detail the horrors committed by Hitler and his Nazi officials. It was these documents that ultimately incriminated Hans von Dohnanyi, Admiral Canaris, General Oster, Dietrich, and the others involved in the conspiracy.

It took years to unravel what had happened to these documents. First they had been hidden in a safe in a deep cellar in Zossen. Christine von Dohnanyi, shortly after she was released from prison, had been assured that the documents no longer existed. She knew, as did the others in the opposition, that if the documents were discovered the Gestapo would learn enough to convict and execute the conspirators. And that is exactly what happened. The documents were not destroyed. It turned out that General Beck felt that the documents were historically important, and those covering the period of 1939–1940 were preserved. In a report written for United States officers during the Nuremberg trials in 1946, Christine von Dohnanyi said that apparently, on General Beck's orders, these files were "readily accessible in Zossen."[14] An officer whose name was known to both Hans and Christine revealed the location of the documents. Neither ever revealed the name of the suspected traitor. However, the discovery of these files was instrumental in the trials and death sentences handed down on the *Abwehr* group, including those of Dietrich, Hans von Dohnanyi, Justus Perels, Hans Oster, and Wilhelm Canaris.

It was in August of 1944 that Hans von Dohnanyi was transferred to a concentration camp, and the family worked out the plan for Dietrich's escape from prison. Corporal Knobloch, a guard who was devoted to Dietrich, wanted to take Dietrich out of the prison gate when he left one afternoon and hide him in some safe place. Rüdiger and Ursula Schleicher and their daughter Renate Bethge secretly met Knobloch to give him a mechanic's uniform as a disguise for Dietrich and some money and food coupons. Everyone expected the escape to take place in early October. But when his brother Klaus was arrested on October 1, 1944, Dietrich refused to escape. An escape, he felt, would only make life more difficult for Klaus, his parents, and his fiancée. A few days later Rüdiger Schleicher was arrested too, and the arrest of Dietrich's friends Justus Perels and Eberhard Bethge soon followed.

Dietrich's last letter to Eberhard was dated August 23, 1944. In that letter he reaffirms his faith in God and adds, "I'm most thankful for the people I have met, and I only hope that they never have to grieve about me, but that they, too, will always be certain of and thankful for God's mercy and forgiveness."[15]

19

The Last Days

O N OCTOBER 8, 1944, Dietrich was secretly moved from Tegel Prison to an S.S. prison in the Prinz Albrecht Strasse in Berlin. For four months he was held prisoner in the basement of this notorious Military Interrogation Prison. All of the conspirators, Sack, Perels, Canaris, Oster, and Beck, had been arrested and by the fall of 1944 were in solitary confinement. The discovery of the Zossen files truly spelled disaster for Dietrich and the others. According to Eberhard Bethge, the Zossen files were turned over to a Gestapo lawyer, Walter Huppenkothen, with instructions to use the files to find evidence that could serve as the basis of further interrogations. The incriminating evidence was compiled into a report, and one copy was sent to Hitler, one to Himmler, and the other was sent to S.S. leaders Kaltenbrunner and Müller. Dietrich Bonhoeffer was one of those targeted for special investigation, as were Canaris, Oster, Dohnanyi, Sack, and Josef Müller. The case against these men never reached the People's Court, but remained under the special concern of Hitler himself. It was Hitler who made the final decision to execute them in April 1945.

Most of the prisoners held in the Gestapo prison at Prinz Albrecht Strasse were tortured. There is no evidence that Dietrich was tortured, although his treatment was far from humane. The cells were small and contained only a table, a stool, and a fold-up bed. The prison heating system gave out in early February. During his four months at the prison on Prinz Albrecht Strasse, Dietrich was allowed to write only three letters. There was a Christmas letter to Maria, a short birthday letter to his mother dated December 28, 1944, and a letter to his parents dated January 17, 1945. This last letter was a brief greeting and included a request for a few simple supplies: toothpaste, some matches, coffee beans, and some specific books including *Lives of Great Men* by Plutarch.

In the beginning of February 1945 Dietrich was moved again. His family did not discover he had been moved until nearly a week later when they came to deliver a package. Maria von Wedemeyer traveled from concentration camp to concentration camp looking for him until she had to abandon the search for Dietrich to help her own family flee from the fighting on the Russian front in Pomerania.

Dietrich's letter of December 19 was to Maria. It contained the poem "By the Powers for Good," as his Christmas greeting to his fiancée, his parents, and his brothers and sisters. Like his other poems, this one contains elements of prayer and praise. The last stanza expresses Dietrich's abiding faith:

> The forces for good surround us in wonder,
> They firm up our courage for what comes our way,
> God's with us from dawn to the slumber of evening,
> The promise of love at the break of each day.[1]

Despite the constant bombing, the shortage of food, and the cruelty of the prison guards, Dietrich was able to see "forces for good" and to find "courage for what comes our way." Courage would be needed to face the dark days ahead. In spite of the notorious conditions at the prison, Dietrich somehow managed to get books and writing materials so that he was able to continue his work in his cell. Unfortunately, the work did not survive the war.

The Allied bombing of Germany intensified in these last years of the war. In March 1942 British bombers attached Lübeck, destroying 1,425 buildings and killing 320 people. In July of 1943,

British planes bombed Hamburg, killing 30,482 people and destroying 3,212 businesses, 24 hospitals, 227 schools, and 58 churches. Bombing raids on Berlin also resulted in destruction, and the Berliners faced air raids almost nightly. The prisoners, Dietrich among them, shared the danger of bombing with the rest of the city. For Dietrich these air raids, both night and day, allowed precious opportunities to visit with other prisoners. One such prisoner was Fabian von Schlabrendorff, a cousin of Maria von Wedemeyer and a Bonhoeffer family friend who had been arrested while fighting for the German army on the Russian front on the suspicion that he was involved in the assassination attempt on Hitler. Schlabrendorff and Dietrich, both of whom were in solitary confinement, used the air raids as a chance to visit. Even the crashing of bombs outside the prison could not dull the joy of their conversation. It was such an air raid evacuation that provided Dietrich a chance to see Hans von Dohnanyi one last time.

Outside contact was no longer possible, but Dietrich had discovered through the prison information network that Hans von Dohnanyi was in the same prison. Fabian von Schlabrendorff reported that

> when we returned after an air-raid warning from our cement shelter, his brother-in-law lay on a stretcher in his cell, paralysed in both legs. With an alacrity that nobody would have believed him capable of, Dietrich Bonhoeffer suddenly dived into the open cell of his brother-in-law. It seemed a miracle that none of the warders saw it. But Dietrich also succeeded in the more difficult part of his venture, in emerging from Dohnanyi's cell unnoticed and getting into line with the column of prisoners who were filing along the corridor.[2]

During this short and dangerous visit, they were able to discuss the important points of the ongoing interrogations.

In the later days of the war air raids often caused severe damage to the prison and great distress to the prisoners. The prisoners were rushed to a cement shelter in the prison yard. The Gestapo were not worried about the prisoners' welfare; rather they wanted to complete the interrogations. Schlabrendorff also recalls that on the night of February 3, 1945, an air raid nearly destroyed the prison.

> Tightly squeezed together we were standing in our air-raid shelter when a bomb hit it with an enormous explosion. For a second it seemed as if the shelter were bursting and the ceiling crashing down on top of us. It rocked like a ship tossing in the storm, but it held.[3]

Dietrich remained "quite calm, he did not move a muscle, but stood motionless and relaxed as if nothing had happened." Dietrich's actions calmed those around him. He acted like a man totally confident that nothing, not even death, could harm him.

On February 7, 1945, Dietrich was moved to the Buchenwald concentration camp, but this information was also withheld from his family. In Buchenwald he was imprisoned in the basement of an S.S. barrack outside of the concentration camp gates. Although he was imprisoned at Buchenwald for almost two months, it is unlikely that he ever saw the inside of the camp. He made friends with a number of fellow political prisoners including Captain Payne Best of the British Secret Service. After the war, Payne Best recalled that "Bonhoeffer was different; just quite calm and normal, seemingly perfectly at his ease . . . his soul really shown in the dark desperation of our prison."[4] On Easter Day, April 1, the prisoners rejoiced, not only because it was Easter but because they could hear American guns approaching. Soon Germany would be liberated.

For Dietrich, though, that liberation would come too late. During the next few days he was moved to the death camp at Flossenbürg. The journey there was not direct, and Dietrich and his fellow prisoners spent a few days traveling to southern Germany and finally arrived in the village of Schönberg. They were taken to a schoolhouse, where they visited together, enjoyed the view of the countryside, and ate plentifully thanks to the generosity of the villagers. One of the prisoners asked Dietrich to lead them in a morning worship service, but Dietrich declined. He knew that several of the prisoners were Catholic, and one, Wassili Kokorin was an atheist. However, when Kokorin spoke in favor of the service,

Dietrich relented. There seemed to be reason for celebration. Everyone assumed that there would be no more trials and that the war would soon be over.

Moments after that service ended, however, two men arrived at the prison, marched into the room and announced, "Prisoner Bonhoeffer, take your things and come with us."[5] Everyone knew that execution usually followed such a command.

Dietrich quickly gathered up his few belongings and said farewell to his fellow prisoners. Using a blunt pencil he wrote his name and address in the front, back, and middle of his copy of *Plutarch* in the hopes that someone might pick it up and be able to trace his movements. (A fellow prisoner retrieved it and returned it to the Bonhoeffer family several years later.) He managed to speak briefly with Payne Best, the British prisoner and asked him to greet Bishop Bell on his return to England. According to Best, Dietrich's parting words were, "This is the end—for me the beginning of life."[6]

Dietrich was transported to Flossenbürg concentration camp. His execution had probably been ordered on April 5 by Hitler during a midday discussion. Throughout the night he and other conspirators were put on trial in an effort to extract further information. Admiral Canaris, General Oster, Karl Sack, Ludwig Gehre, Theodor Strunck, and Dietrich Bonhoeffer were sentenced to death by their interrogators.

At 6:00 A.M. on April 9, 1945, the prisoners were taken from their cells and their verdicts read aloud. The prison doctor watched as Dietrich Bonhoeffer knelt in prayer. "I was most deeply moved by the way this lovable man prayed, so devout and so certain that God heard his prayer." He prayed again as he approached the gallows, and then climbed the steps, "brave and composed."[7]

20

Heritage of Faith

Beyond 1945

L ESS THAN A MONTH LATER, the war was over, but weeks
    passed as Eberhard searched for news of Dietrich. It was
    Sabine, Dietrich's sister, who was the first to learn of her
brother's death. On May 31, 1945, Julius Rieger, a German pastor
living in England, delivered the news. Sabine had no way to get
word to the family in Germany.

Maria von Wedemeyer, who traveled to the western part of Germany in search of Dietrich, didn't learn the news until June.

Eberhard Bethge and Dietrich's parents did not receive word
until July 27, 1945, when British radio broadcast a memorial service for Dietrich which was held in London. Bishop Bell, Franz
Hildebrandt, and Julius Rieger conducted the service. In his sermon Bishop Bell said:

> Wherever he [Dietrich] went and whoever he spoke with—
> whether young or old—he was fearless, regardless of himself, and
> with it all, devoted heart and soul to his parents, his friends, his
> country as God willed it to be, to his Church and to his Master.[1]

When the Bonhoeffers learned that others in the *Abwehr* group,
including Oster and Canaris, had been sentenced to death and
hanged, they assumed that Hans von Dohnanyi had been killed in

the Sachsenhausen concentration camp as well. It was not until the War Trials in 1949 and 1956 that they learned more about the death sentence of Hans von Dohnanyi. Sources located in 1997 finally confirmed April 9 as Hans von Dohnanyi's execution date.

The Bonhoeffer family paid dearly for their courageous resistance to Hitler. Two brothers, Dietrich and Klaus, and two brothers-in-law, Rüdiger Schleicher and Hans von Dohnanyi, were killed by the Gestapo. Daughter Sabine and her family were forced into exile in England and could not return to Germany until 1947. The health and welfare of daughters Ursula and Christine and all the grandchildren were in constant danger during the long months of waiting and constant air raids. The saving grace was the sure knowledge that the men died for a noble cause.

The years after the war were difficult for the Bonhoeffer family. The memories remained, of course, and so did the letters—letters to the family, letters to Maria von Wedemeyer, letters to Eberhard Bethge—and it is through the letters that the world came to know Dietrich Bonhoeffer. In 1945, however, the world knew nothing of Dietrich Bonhoeffer. In the words of Eberhard Bethge, "In 1945, only a handful of friends and enemies knew who this young man had been; the names of other Christians in Germany were more in the limelight."[2] Eberhard began his life's work modestly. He felt it was his duty to his friend to draw together the fragments of *Ethics* and bring them to publication. It has since been restructured and reworked several times.

It was the publication of the letters in 1953 that brought Dietrich Bonhoeffer to the attention of the world. In an essay titled, "How the Prison Letters Survived,"[3] Eberhard Bethge tells the story of the correspondence, his efforts to preserve the letters, and of his arrest and escape from prison. He was eventually able to gather together all of the letters except for the few that were lost to dampness or that Eberhard himself destroyed just moments before his own arrest. He writes, "Seven years later we held in our hands a selection of his letters from prison in the form of a book . . . And we began to be amazed at the response they evoked around the world.[4] The first edition was in German, but the book was soon translated into English for American and British readers, and eventually *Letters and Papers from Prison* was translated into sixteen languages. It has never gone out of print and is now available to readers throughout the world. In the original edition only Dietrich's letters were published. Not until 1997 did a revised edition appear in English which included the letters to Dietrich as well as from him. This later edition provides a more complete glimpse into the nature of the dialogue between Eberhard and Dietrich. The revised edition also included fragments of novels and a drama, as well as several poems. Dietrich's poems surprised and delighted Eberhard Bethge when he first received them. They have inspired Christians throughout the world. One of the poems, "By Gracious Powers," has been set to music and is included in the hymnbooks of many religious denominations.

The beautiful love letters that Dietrich wrote to Maria were withheld at her request until her death. They were published in 1992 by her sister, Ruth-Alice von Bismarck under the title *Love Letters from Cell 92*. These letters reveal the joy with which Dietrich looked forward to his life with Maria. On August 12, 1943, Dietrich wrote to Maria, "Our marriage shall be a yes to God's earth; it shall strengthen our courage to act and accomplish something on earth."[5] These letters also expose the gulf in their ages and experiences, but that Maria was a brilliant young woman is evident from her responses and the nature of their correspondence. Maria kept the letters private. In a letter to her sister written several years after Dietrich's death, she said, "It always surprises me how incredibly sensitive I am in regard to Dietrich and my relationship with him."[6] Thanks to the work of Maria's sister, Ruth-Alice von Bismarck, the letters are now available to readers around the world.

In the following years, Eberhard Bethge edited other works by Dietrich Bonhoeffer under the title *Collected Works*. Eberhard was concerned about the way in which some theologians were distorting ideas from the prison letters. He felt that they needed to see Bonhoeffer's writing in context. In 1986, the German publisher Chr. Kaiser Verlag, issued the first of a sixteen-volume edition of the *Dietrich Bonhoeffer Werke*. The International Bonhoeffer Society has undertaken the responsibility for translating all sixteen volumes into English.

In 1967 Eberhard Bethge completed a biography, *Dietrich Bon-*

hoeffer: Man of Vision, Man of Courage, and later, with his wife, Renate, he created a picture biography to reach an even wider audience. After Dietrich's death, Eberhard remembered a casual conversation:

> Perhaps the process of becoming his biographer began when, at the beginning of the war, Bonhoeffer said in jest that I should carefully note something that he had just said—of course, I have now completely forgotten what it was—so that I might one day have something to write about him. At the time I did not imagine for one moment that the course of events would really make me his biographer one day.[7]

Eberhard Bethge was, of course, more than Dietrich Bonhoeffer's biographer. Their remarkable friendship grew stronger as they moved beyond the church struggles and into the conspiracy. Eberhard helped Dietrich to focus and refine his theological work and enabled him to carry to publication the work that Dietrich considered so important, *Ethics*. Eberhard devoted his life's work to preserving the ideas and ideals of his best friend, Dietrich Bonhoeffer.

Eberhard Bethge helped theologians understand the complex ideas presented, but not fully developed, in the prison letters. Several of the concepts that the two men discussed in their letters have confused modern scholars. Through his life Dietrich focused on the difficult question of what Christianity really is, or indeed who Christ really is, for us today. He had asked the same questions earlier as a student, a young pastor, a pacifist, and as a political activist committed to stopping the madman and sparing God's people more suffering. He gradually came to see the need for Christians to move beyond traditional church structures. The German Christians preserved the appearance of church, but it was a church without God. Dietrich Bonhoeffer believed in a God who suffers with people and who acts with love and forgiveness toward people.

Every day his faith seemed to grow stronger as did his belief that to live as a Christian means to live for others. In May 1944 he penned a special baptism letter to his namesake, Eberhard and Renate Bethge's son, Dietrich Wilhelm Rüdiger Bethge. He wrote of the future that young Dietrich would face: "being Christians today will be limited to two things: prayer and action for justice on behalf of people. All Christian thinking, speaking, and organizing must be born anew out of this prayer and action."[8]

Dietrich Bonhoeffer has influenced Christians and non-Christians throughout the world, not only through his theology but through his life and actions. It is impossible to count the individuals who have been strengthened and encouraged by his example of Christian love and compassion—and his influence extended from individuals to groups and movements in places as far apart as Latin America, Korea, and South Africa. In an article in the *Princeton Seminary Bulletin* in 2001, theologian Beatriz Melano discussed Bonhoeffer's influence on Latin American theologians during the time of repressive dictatorships in Brazil and Argentina. Melano directly credits the formation of the ISAL (Church and Society in Latin America) movement to Bonhoeffer's works and witness. It was through this movement that many Christians in South America were able to fight for social justice and human rights. "Our protest marches were vigorous, yet peaceful, and our theological teaching concentrated on the moment in history in which we were living," she writes.

> It was Bonhoeffer's example, mediated to us through Paul Lehmann, that gave us faith and courage when the police interrogated us in our homes and in the jails, inventoried our personal libraries, and falsely accused many of us of being "subversives" and "communists."[9]

Melano writes that it is Bonhoeffer's pacifism and ethic of self-sacrifice that inspired these Latin American Christians.

In South Africa too, the work and witness of Dietrich Bonhoeffer exerted a positive influence for peace and compassion. South African theologian John W. De Gruchy has spoken and written extensively on the influence of Bonhoeffer on his country. His is a nuanced argument that recognizes the many differences between South Africa's struggle with apartheid and Germany's struggle with anti-Semitism, but he recognizes that Bonhoeffer had a forceful impact on South African Christians who began to listen to their black neighbors, recognized the legitimacy of their struggle for independence, and then identified, as best they were able, with that struggle.

Theologian John D. Godsey has spoken about Bonhoeffer's influence on Christians in West Africa, Cuba, and Korea, and in 1996 a young Korean theologian identified Bonhoeffer as "the major theological mentor" of the Korean Student Christian movement.[10] Theologian Victoria J. Barnett observed in 1995 that

> Bonhoeffer's thought has inspired several generations of German theology students, African-Americans, Latin American Catholics, South Korean activists, and many others. Fifty years after his death, this German Lutheran still has something to say.[11]

While the problems facing Latin America, Korea, and South Africa were totally different from those facing Germany in the 1930s and 1940s, Bonhoeffer has been crucial in helping people throughout the world, including civil rights activists in the United States, to realize that obeying God's commands means helping the weak and the suffering, no matter the cost. In *The Cost of Discipleship*, he wrote, "any attack even on the least of people is an attack on Christ, who took human form, and in his own person restored the image of God in all that bears a human form."[12] Bonhoeffer asked Christians to return to the teachings of the gospel. He asked that Christians become partners with the suffering God. "We are summoned," he writes, "to share in God's sufferings at the hands of a godless world."[13]

Dietrich Bonhoeffer never abandoned his belief that prayer, Bible reading, and worship empowered people to live in the world as servants of Jesus Christ. In his poem "Christians and Pagans," written in July of 1944, immediately after the failed coup, he expressed his belief that while God loves and cares for everyone, Christians love and care for God when they reach out to those who are "poor, scorned, without shelter or bread."[14] For Dietrich Bonhoeffer "standing steadfast by God" meant living in the real world. It meant standing side by side with all God's people, Jew or Gentile, and suffering with all who suffer. It also meant planning for a future without war, a world in which we not only pray for peace, but achieve it.

Afterword

What Happened to Family and Friends

After 1945

I N THE WEEKS AND MONTHS immediately after the war, the Bonhoeffer family concentrated on providing food, shelter, and comfort to the children now left without fathers. It took time until the role of those involved in the opposition against Hitler was acknowledged and generally accepted, and their widows did not receive the widow's pension to which they were entitled until years later. In the meantime, they had to find ways to provide for the children. Slowly life returned to more normal routines, but for those involved in the conspiracy, life had been changed forever.

In the last days of the war, extensive bombing had caused serious damage to many of the Bonhoeffer family homes. On April 23, 1945, the home of Klaus and Emmi Bonhoeffer was destroyed by a bomb. Emmi, who was living there alone, escaped injury and ran to the Bonhoeffer parents' house, a half-hour away. During the Battle of Berlin, Emmi and the elder Bonhoeffers found safety in the cellar of the Schleichers' home next door. When Emmi received the word that Klaus had been shot in the last days of the war, she set out to reach her three children, who had been staying with friends in the comparative safety of rural Germany. It took her two weeks travel by bicycle and on foot before she reached them, and then she had the hard task of telling them of their father's death.

Emmi Bonhoeffer reported that a New York clergyman drew up a list of resistance fighters. Church members in the United States began sending packages of clothing in 1947. The thank-you letters that she wrote were published in the United States, without her knowledge, and more packages arrived. She exchanged the clothes for food whenever possible, and eventually began a program of paying workers in clothes. It was in this manner that she managed to help many others and even arranged the paving of a main thoroughfare. This experience led to additional work in refugee resettlement. When the war trials began in 1963, Emmi Bonhoeffer traveled to Frankfurt to provide aid and comfort to the Auschwitz survivors who had been called to testify. Her book *Auschwitz Trials: Letters from an Eyewitness* (Richmond, Va.: John Knox Press, 1967) is based on these experiences. Eventually she became active in Amnesty International. Emmi Bonhoeffer died on March 12, 1991, in Düsseldorf, Germany.

Ursula Schleicher's home had been the center of support for the men in prison. She organized the preparation of food and supply packages and supervised their delivery amid the almost constant air raids and attacks of 1945. Her home was heavily damaged by a bomb on April 27, 1945, and she suffered from exhaustion and heart problems, which grew worse after the devastating news of her husband's death. In 1947 she supervised the rebuilding of the house and, after her father's death a year later, she cared for her aging mother. In 1961 she moved from Berlin to Hamburg, where she was always available to help her children and enjoyed frequent visits with her ten grandchildren. She died in 1983.

Christine von Dohnanyi, who had been imprisoned for five weeks in 1943 by the Gestapo, devoted herself to her children's welfare after the war. Because her house on the outskirts of Berlin fell within the Russian zone after the war, she moved her family to Munich, where she had friends. She, too, suffered from heart problems and died in 1965.

Dietrich's parents remained strong in the immediate aftermath of the war as they helped their daughters and daughter-in-law support the grandchildren. Their home was a haven for Ursula's family and others needing shelter. In March 1948, the remaining family was reunited for Karl Bonhoeffer's eightieth birthday and the celebration of the fiftieth wedding anniversary of Karl and Paula Bonhoeffer. A few months later, on December 4, 1948, Karl Bonhoeffer died of a stroke. Paula, his wife, died on February 1, 1951, at the age of seventy-four.

Sabine Leibholz and her family remained in England until 1947, when Sabine and Gerhard were able to return to Germany to visit with family. Sabine, who as a child enjoyed art, became an artist and sculptor in later life. She died in 1999.

The youngest sister, Susi, who had married Confessing Church pastor Walter Dress, remained in Berlin throughout her life. During the war she provided shelter, food, and clothing to several Jewish families. After the war, she collected money to help the wounded, particularly those who needed prosthetic limbs. She died in 1991.

Karl-Friedrich, who had fought in World War I and was too old to be conscripted for military service during the Third Reich, was the only Bonhoeffer son to survive the war. He spent as much time as possible with his aging parents after the war and died of a heart attack in 1957 at the age of fifty-eight.

After the war, Maria von Wedemeyer, Dietrich's fiancée, began college work at Göttingen University. Her sister, visiting her in 1946, recalled that Dietrich was her only topic of conversation. As soon as it was possible, Maria traveled to Berlin for a bittersweet reunion with the Bonhoeffer family. She cherished contacts with them throughout her life. After Maria's move to America, Emmi Bonhoeffer and Eberhard and Renate Bethge visited her whenever they were in the United States.

In 1948 Maria traveled to Bryn Mawr College in the United States to continue her study of mathematics. As a mathematician, she became involved in the early development of computers and worked for both Remington Rand and Honeywell corporations. Maria married twice and had two sons, both of whom were born in the United States. Throughout her life Maria kept her letters from Dietrich private. Shortly before her death on November 16,

1977, she entrusted the letters to her sister, Ruth-Alice von Bismarck, and gave permission for their publication. Ruth-Alice von Bismarck published them under the title *Love Letters from Cell 92: The Correspondence between Dietrich Bonhoeffer and Maria von Wedemeyer, 1943–45.*

Dietrich's friend Franz Hildebrandt remained in England. He had married in 1943 and had become a Methodist minister. In 1953 Hildebrandt accepted a position as a theology professor at Drew University Theological School in Madison, New Jersey. He remained in the United States until 1968. He spent his later years as a pastor in Scotland, where he died in 1985.

Eberhard Bethge continued throughout his life to serve as Dietrich Bonhoeffer's biographer and theological interpreter. Immediately after the war, Bethge worked for the newly reestablished German Evangelical Church in Berlin. In 1953 he moved his family to London, where he served for eight years as pastor of the same congregation served by Dietrich Bonhoeffer from 1934 to 1935. Bethge also spent time at Union Seminary in New York and as a seminary director in Germany. He traveled the world, attending meetings of the International Bonhoeffer Society, visiting seminaries and universities, and seeking to encourage and support conversations between Jews and Christians. Eberhard Bethge died on March 18, 2000, in the home he shared with Renate, his wife of fifty-seven years.

Chronology of Events
in Dietrich Bonhoeffer's Life

1906   Dietrich and twin sister, Sabine, are born on February 4.

1912   Bonhoeffer family moves to Berlin.

1913   Dietrich begins formal schooling at the Friedrich Werder school.

1916   Family moves into a home at 14 Wangenheimstrasse, Grunewald, Berlin.

1918   Walter, Dietrich's older brother, dies of war wounds.

1921   Dietrich and Sabine are confirmed at the Grunewald Church in Berlin.

1923   Dietrich begins his university studies at Tübingen.

1924   Dietrich and Klaus travel to Rome and North Africa.

1927   Dietrich completes and defends his doctoral thesis, *The Communion of Saints*. He receives his licentiate in theology.

1928   Dietrich is appointed assistant pastor of a German congregation in Barcelona, Spain.

1929   Dietrich lectures in systematic theology at Berlin University.

1930   Dietrich completes a second thesis, *Act and Being*. It is accepted as the required dissertation to allow him to become a regular university lecturer. In September, he leaves for the United States to study theology at Union Seminary in New York City.

1931   In May and June, Dietrich travels to Mexico with a fellow student, Jean Lasserre. After he returns to Germany, he meets Karl Barth in Bonn. In August, Dietrich is appointed lecturer in theology at Berlin University.

1931   In September, he is appointed youth secretary for the World Alliance for Promoting International Friendship through the Churches at a conference in England. In October, he is appointed chaplain at the Technical College in Berlin. He is ordained as a Lutheran pastor in November and begins teaching confirmation classes at Zion Church in Berlin.

1932   He teaches at Berlin University.

1933   Dietrich publishes essay "The Church and the Jewish Problem." In October, he moves to London and becomes pastor of two German churches there. He meets Bishop George K. A. Bell of Chichester, England.

1934   In August, Dietrich attends the Ecumenical Conference at Fanö, Denmark. In December, he visits several Anglican monasteries in England.

1935   He returns to Germany to accept a position as Director of the Confessing Church seminary at Finkenwalde (now in Poland). His parents move to 43 Marienburger Allee in Charlottenburg, Berlin.

1936   Dietrich is disqualified from teaching at Berlin University.

1937   Dietrich attends ecumenical meeting in London and resigns as youth secretary. In September, the seminary at Finkenwalde is closed by Gestapo. *The Cost of Discipleship* is published. Dietrich begins the collective pastorates in Koslin and Gross-Schlönwitz.

1938   In January, Dietrich is forbidden to work in Berlin. In February, he first meets Resistance leaders Canaris, Oster, Beck, and Sack. He helps his sister Sabine and her family escape to England by way of Switzerland. He writes *Life Together*.

1939   Dietrich travels to London to meet with Bishop Bell, Reinhold Niebuhr, and Willem Visser 't Hooft. In June, he travels to United States, but returns in July. By August, he has become a civilian agent of the *Abwehr*, German military intelligence agency.

1940   The Gestapo closes the seminary in Koslin and Gross-Schlönwitz. In September, Dietrich is prohibited from speaking in public and must report regularly to the Gestapo. He begins writing *Ethics*. In November, he joins the *Abwehr* staff in Munich.

1941 Dietrich travels to Switzerland to visit Karl Barth and Willem Visser 't Hooft in February. He visits Switzerland again in August.

1942 Dietrich travels to Norway and Sweden with Helmuth von Moltke on counterespionage mission. In May, he returns to Switzerland for a third time.

1943 In January, Dietrich becomes engaged to Maria von Wedemeyer. On April 5, he is arrested and imprisoned at Tegel Prison in Berlin. He is interrogated in prison in July. He is able to begin a correspondence with Eberhard Bethge in November.

1944 In March, heavy bombing occurs over Tegel Prison. In October, Dietrich is moved to Gestapo prison at Prinz-Albrecht-Strasse, Berlin.

1945 February 7, Dietrich is moved to Buchenwald concentration camp. April 3, he is moved to Regensburg. April 6, he is moved to Schonberg. April 8, he is moved to Flossenbürg concentration camp and court-martialed. April 9, Dietrich Bonhoeffer is murdered at Flossenbürg. July 27, a memorial service for Dietrich is held in London and broadcast to Germany. This is the first word his parents receive of his death.

1949 Dietrich's writings are collected and edited by Eberhard Bethge and published under the title *Ethics*.

1953 *Letters and Papers from Prison* is published by Eberhard Bethge.

1957 First edition of *Dietrich Bonhoeffer: Man of Vision, Man of Courage* by Eberhard Bethge is published in Germany.

1995 *Love Letters from Cell 92: The Correspondence between Dietrich Bonhoeffer and Maria von Wedemeyer, 1943–45*, is published.

2000 Revised edition of *Dietrich Bonhoeffer: A Biography* by Eberhard Bethge is published in the United States. Bethge dies on March 18, 2000.

Glossary

Abwehr   The Counterintelligence Office of the High Command of the Armed Forces in Germany. The *Abwehr* became the center of the German resistance movement against the Nazis. Dietrich Bonhoeffer worked for the *Abwehr* from 1939 until 1943.

Aryan Clause   A law passed by the German government on April 7, 1933, which banned any person whose parents or grandparents were Jewish from government employment.

Barmen Confession   The declaration of faith, written in 1934, adopted by many Protestant church leaders and largely composed by theologian Karl Barth. The confession stated that Jesus Christ alone is Lord, and Christians must not accept the "false teaching that there are . . . other lords."

Bethel Confession   The declaration of faith drafted in 1933 by Dietrich Bonhoeffer and Hermann Sasse. The confession spoke strongly against Hitler's racist policies against the Jewish citizens of Germany. It was revised and so watered down that Bonhoeffer refused to sign the final version.

confirmation   In the Protestant tradition, official recognition as an adult member of a Christian congregation. Young people between age twelve and fourteen usually attend classes to prepare for church membership and are then "confirmed" at a special communion service.

concentration camp   A camp where the Nazis imprisoned persons they considered dangerous. Concentration camps existed throughout Germany and in many of the territories that the German army conquered. Millions of people were sent to such camps: communists, Jews, political resisters, and many Catholic priests and Protestant ministers who refused to cooperate with Hitler's government.

Confessing Church A church group formed in 1934 to protest the claims of the German Christians that the church owed allegiance to Hitler and the Nazis. The founders, members of the Pastors' Emergency League, wanted freedom for the church and declared that Jesus Christ, not Hitler, was Lord.

death camp A camp whose main function was to kill the prisoners. Although the mass killing of Jews began in 1941, most of the death camps came into existence in 1942 in response to Hitler's plan to kill all the Jews, which he called the "Final Solution to the Jewish Problem."

ecumenical A movement that encouraged the unity and cooperation of all Christian churches. Peace was one of the movement's main aims.

Final Solution This term was developed at the Wannsee Conference held on January 20, 1942, as a euphemism for the murder of all European Jews. Plans were developed that Jews from throughout Europe would be gathered in work camps, that most would "fall away" (die) during work projects, and that the remainder would be killed.

Führer The title given to Adolf Hitler, the leader of Nazi Germany.

German Christians Pastors and members of Protestant churches who pledged support to Hitler and accepted the Aryan Clause.

German Evangelical Church The state church of Germany, which included both Lutheran and Reformed congregations. Taxes supported the churches, and pastors were considered employees of the government.

Gestapo Hitler's secret police. They conducted illegal searches, seized evidence, and interrogated those suspected of opposing the Nazi government.

Pastors' Emergency League The organization of pastors that developed from the Young Reformers. This organization hoped to counter the activities of the German Christians.

S.A. The abbreviation used for Hitler's storm troopers. The soldiers in this special army were often referred to as "Brownshirts." In the early years of the Third Reich, they often demonstrated outside churches or took part in large public demonstrations of support for Hitler. In 1934 they lost favor with Hitler and many of the leaders were killed.

S.S. This elite squadron began as Hitler's bodyguards. S.S. officers remained separate from the regular German army and were extremely powerful. In addition to other duties, they were in charge of the concentration camps and the death camps.

swastika   This ancient good luck symbol was modified to become the symbol of the Nazis and became a part of the German flag. Wearing a swastika became a sign of support for Hitler and the Third Reich.

Tegel   The Gestapo prison in the heart of Berlin, where political prisoners were held for interrogation.

Third Reich   The name given to Hitler's government, which began in 1933. The word *Reich* means empire. The Nazis traced their history through two other empires prior to Hitler's rule.

Young Reformers   A group of pastors from the German Evangelical Church who joined together to protest the exclusion of people of Jewish descent from the Christian church.

Notes

All Bible quotations are from the New Revised Standard Version.

Chapter 1. The Search for Dietrich Bonhoeffer

1. Eberhard Bethge and Renate Bethge, eds., *Last Letters of the Resistance: Farewells from the Bonhoeffer Family*, p. 27.
2. Ibid., p. 41.
3. Rüdiger Schleicher was the father of Eberhard's wife, Renate.
4. Dorothee von Meding, *Courageous Hearts: Women and the Anti-Hitler Plot of 1944*, p. 22.
5. Dorothee Bracher (daughter of Ursula [Bonhoeffer] Schleicher and niece of Dietrich Bonhoeffer and Hans von Dohnanyi), letter to author, April 1, 1998. Bracher adds, "It was only through the trials held against the Gestapo functionary and S.S. leader Huppenkothen and Gestapo detective Sondregger between 1949 and 1956 that more information about the death sentence of Hans von Dohnanyi came to light, though no definitive date of his execution. New sources, found during the last year among the archives of the former DDR, finally confirmed more definitely the 9th April 1945 as the date for his execution. . . ."
6. Susanne Dress, interviewed on *Dietrich Bonhoeffer: Memories and Perspectives*, produced by Trinity Films, Inc., 1982, 90 min., videocassette.
7. Dietrich Bonhoeffer, *A Testament to Freedom: The Essential Writings of Dietrich Bonhoeffer*, p. 161.
8. Eberhard Bethge, *Dietrich Bonhoeffer: A Biography*, p. 931.
9. Ibid., p. 933.

Chapter 2. Childhood: A Short and Happy Peace

1. Sabine Leibholz-Bonhoeffer, *The Bonhoeffers: Portrait of a Family*, p. 5.

2. Eberhard Bethge, Renate Bethge, and Christian Gremmels, eds., *Dietrich Bonhoeffer: A Life in Pictures*, p. 29.

3. Mary Bosanquet, *The Life and Death of Dietrich Bonhoeffer*, p. 29.

4. Ibid.

5. Emmi Bonhoeffer, "Professors' Children as Neighbors," in *I Knew Dietrich Bonhoeffer*, ed. Wolf-Dieter Zimmermann and Ronald Gregor Smith, p. 36.

6. Bethge, *Dietrich Bonhoeffer: A Biography*, p. 24.

7. Bethge and others, *Dietrich Bonhoeffer: A Life in Pictures*, p. 35.

8. Bethge, *Dietrich Bonhoeffer: A Biography*, p. 20.

9. Wolf-Dieter Zimmermann, interview with the author, July 21, 1998.

10. Dietrich Bonhoeffer, *Letters & Papers from Prison*, new greatly enlarged edition, p. 211.

11. Leibholz-Bonhoeffer, *The Bonhoeffers: Portrait of a Family*, pp. 32–33.

Chapter 3. The First Death

1. Sabine Leibholz, "Childhood and Home," in *I Knew Dietrich Bonhoeffer*, ed. Wolf-Dieter Zimmermann and Ronald Gregor Smith, p. 29.

2. Hans-Christoph von Hase, conversation with author, July 12, 1998.

3. D. Bonhoeffer, *A Testament to Freedom*, p. 189.

4. Ibid., p. 190.

5. Ibid.

6. Emmi Bonhoeffer, "Professors' Children as Neighbors," in *I Knew Dietrich Bonhoeffer*, ed. Wolf-Dieter Zimmermann and Ronald Gregor Smith, p. 36.

7. Bethge, *Dietrich Bonhoeffer: A Biography*, p. 36.

8. Ibid., p. 42.

9. Renate Wind, *Dietrich Bonhoeffer: A Spoke in the Wheel*, p. 25.

Chapter 4. University Days

1. Meding, *Courageous Hearts*, p. 9.

2. D. Bonhoeffer, *A Testament to Freedom*, p. 270.

3. Bethge, *Dietrich Bonhoeffer: A Biography*, p. 50.

4. Ibid., p. 60.

5. Ibid.

6. Hans-Christoph von Hase, interview with the author, July 12, 1998.

7. Bethge, *Dietrich Bonhoeffer: A Biography*, p. 67.

8. Wolf-Dieter Zimmermann, interview with the author, July 21, 1998.

9. Leibholz-Bonhoeffer, *The Bonhoeffers: Portrait of a Family*, p. 13.

10. D. Bonhoeffer, *A Testament to Freedom*, p. 62.

11. Ibid., pp. 62–63.

12. Franz Hildebrandt, "An Oasis of Freedom," in *I Knew Dietrich Bonhoeffer*, ed. Wolf-Dieter Zimmermann and Ronald Gregor Smith, p. 38.

Chapter 5. Barcelona, Spain

1. D. Bonhoeffer, *A Testament to Freedom*, pp. 379–80.

2. Ibid.

3. Leibholz-Bonhoeffer, *The Bonhoeffers: Portrait of a Family*, p. 37.

4. Bethge, *Dietrich Bonhoeffer: A Biography*, p. 134.

5. Ibid., p. 105.

Chapter 6. New York, New York

1. Paul Lehmann, "Paradox of Discipleship," in *I Knew Dietrich Bonhoeffer*, ed. Wolf-Dieter Zimmermann and Ronald Gregor Smith, p. 45.

2. Bethge, *Dietrich Bonhoeffer: A Biography*, p. 150.

3. Ibid., p. 149.

4. D. Bonhoeffer, *A Testament to Freedom*, p. 192.

5. Bosanquet, *Life and Death of Dietrich Bonhoeffer*, p. 84.

6. Paul Lehmann, interviewed on *Dietrich Bonhoeffer: Memories and Perspectives*.

7. Bethge, *Dietrich Bonhoeffer: A Biography*, p. 151.

8. Bosanquet, *Life and Death of Dietrich Bonhoeffer*, p. 87.

9. Marion Lehmann, interviewed on *Dietrich Bonhoeffer: Memories and Perspectives*.

10. Jean Lasserre, interviewed on *Dietrich Bonhoeffer: Memories and Perspectives*.

Chapter 7. Pacifism and Protests

1. Bethge, *Dietrich Bonhoeffer: A Biography*, p. 176.

2. D. Bonhoeffer, *A Testament to Freedom*, p. 383.

3. Ibid., p. 388.

4. Bethge, *Dietrich Bonhoeffer: A Biography*, p. 208.

5. D. Bonhoeffer, *A Testament to Freedom*, p. 95.

6. Ibid., pp. 424–25.

7. Dietrich Bonhoeffer, *No Rusty Swords*, pp. 123–24.

8. Bethge, *Dietrich Bonhoeffer: A Biography*, p. 234.

9. D. Bonhoeffer, *A Testament to Freedom*, p. 384.

10. Richard Rother, "A Confirmation Class in Wedding," in *I Knew Dietrich Bonhoeffer*, ed. Wolf-Dieter Zimmermann and Ronald Gregor Smith, p. 57.

11. Jackson J. Spielvogel, *Hitler and Nazi Germany: A History*, p. 132.

12. Ibid., p. 131.

13. Ibid., p. 132.

14. Franz Hildebrandt, "An Oasis of Freedom," in *I Knew Dietrich Bonhoeffer*, ed. Wolf-Dieter Zimmermann and Ronald Gregor Smith, p. 38.

Chapter 8. Speaking Out

1. Bethge, *Dietrich Bonhoeffer: A Biography*, p. 260.

2. D. Bonhoeffer, *No Rusty Swords*, p. 202.

3. Bethge, *Dietrich Bonhoeffer: A Biography*, p. 263.

4. Renate Bethge and Dorothee Bracher, conversation with author, Bonn, Germany, July 10, 1998.

5. Stephen A. Wise, "Why Isn't Bonhoeffer Honored at Yad Vashem?" *Christianity Today*, February 25, 1998, p. 202.

6. Ernst Christian Helmreich, *The German Churches under Hitler: Background, Struggle, and Epilogue*, p. 138.

7. D. Cajus Fabricius, *Positive Christianity in the Third Reich*, p. 19.

8. For a detailed understanding of the German Christian movement, see Doris L. Bergen, *Twisted Cross: The German Christian Movement in the Third Reich*.

9. Helmreich, *The German Churches under Hitler*, p. 138.

10. D. Bonhoeffer, *A Testament to Freedom*, p. 132.

11. Kenneth C. Barnes, "Dietrich Bonhoeffer and Hitler's Persecution of the Jews," in *Betrayal: German Churches and the Holocaust*, ed. Robert P. Ericksen and Susannah Heschel, p. 114.

12. D. Bonhoeffer, *No Rusty Swords*, p. 228.

13. Leibholz-Bonhoeffer, *The Bonhoeffers: Portrait of a Family*, p. 75.

14. Hans-Werner Jensen, "Life Together," in *I Knew Dietrich Bonhoeffer*, ed. Wolf-Dieter Zimmermann and Ronald Gregor Smith, p. 154.

Chapter 9. The Church Elections

1. Bethge, *Dietrich Bonhoeffer: A Biography*, p. 290.

2. Ibid., p. 296.

3. Klaus Scholder, *The Churches and the Third Reich*, p. 446.

4. Bethge, *Dietrich Bonhoeffer: A Biography*, p. 299.

5. D. Bonhoeffer, *A Testament to Freedom*, p. 419.

6. Ibid.

7. Ibid., p. 136.

8. D. Bonhoeffer, *No Rusty Swords*, pp. 235–36.

9. Bethge, *Dietrich Bonhoeffer: A Biography*, p. 314.

10. Ibid., p. 315.

Chapter 10. England

1. Amos Cresswell and Maxwell Tow, *Dr. Franz Hildebrandt: Mr. Valiant-For-Truth*, pp. 122–23.

2. Martin Gilbert, *The Holocaust: A History of the Jews of Europe During the Second World War*, p. 61.

3. Leonidas E. Hill, "The Nazi Attack on 'un-German' Literature, 1933-1945," in *The Holocaust and the Book: Destruction and Preservation*, ed. Jonathan Rose, p. 17.

4. D. Bonhoeffer, *No Rusty Swords*, p. 256.

5. Helmreich, *The German Churches under Hitler*, p. 149.

6. James Bentley, *Martin Niemöller: 1892–1984*, p. 79.

7. Bethge, *Dietrich Bonhoeffer: A Biography*, p. 335.

8. Cresswell and Tow, *Dr. Franz Hildebrandt*, p. 63.

9. D. Bonhoeffer, *No Rusty Swords*, pp. 291–92.

10. Otto Dudzus, "Arresting the Wheel," in *I Knew Dietrich Bonhoeffer*, ed. Wolf-Dieter Zimmermann and Ronald Gregor Smith, p. 90.

11. Bethge, *Dietrich Bonhoeffer: A Biography*, p. 407.

Chapter 11. Finkenwalde

1. Eberhard Bethge, *Friendship and Resistance: Essays on Dietrich Bonhoeffer*, p. 4.

2. Leibholz-Bonhoeffer, *The Bonhoeffers: Portrait of a Family*, p. 42.

3. Bethge, *Friendship and Resistance*, p. 5.

4. Wolf-Dieter Zimmermann, "Finkenwalde," in *I Knew Dietrich Bonhoeffer*, ed. Wolf-Dieter Zimmermann and Ronald Gregor Smith, p. 109.

5. Bethge, *Dietrich Bonhoeffer: A Biography*, p. 429.

6. Werner Koch, "Dietrich Bonhoeffer in Pomerania," in *I Knew Dietrich Bonhoeffer*, ed. Wolf-Dieter Zimmermann and Ronald Gregor Smith, p. 115.

Chapter 12. Protests and Persecution

1. Johannes Goebel, "When He Sat Down at the Piano," in *I Knew Dietrich Bonhoeffer*, ed. Wolf-Dieter Zimmermann and Ronald Gregor Smith, p. 124.

2. D. Bonhoeffer, *A Testament to Freedom*, p. 166.

3. Bethge, *Dietrich Bonhoeffer: A Biography*, p. 498.

4. Emmi Bonhoeffer, interviewed in *Dietrich Bonhoeffer: Memories and Perspectives*.

5. D. Bonhoeffer, *A Testament to Freedom*, p. 161.

6. Ibid., p. 314.

7. Ibid., p. 308.

8. D. Bonhoeffer, *The Cost of Discipleship*, p. 91.

9. "Books of the Century: Leaders and Thinkers Weigh In On the Top 10," *Christianity Today*, April 24, 2000, p. 92.

10. J. S. Conway, "The German Church Struggle: Its Making and Meaning," in *The Church Confronts the Nazis*, ed. Hubert G. Locke, 131.

Chapter 13. The Secret Seminaries

1. Leibholz-Bonhoeffer, *The Bonhoeffers: Portrait of a Family*, pp. 86–87.

2. D. Bonhoeffer, *A Testament to Freedom*, p. 324.

3. Bethge, *Dietrich Bonhoeffer: A Biography*, p. 591.

4. Ibid., p. 593.

5. Gottfried Maltusch, "When the Synagogues Burnt," in *I Knew Dietrich Bonhoeffer*, ed. Wolf-Dieter Zimmermann and Ronald Gregor Smith, p. 150.

Chapter 14. Dangerous Secrets

1. Bethge, *Dietrich Bonhoeffer: A Biography*, p. 625.

2. Winfried Maechler, interviewed in *Dietrich Bonhoeffer: Memories and Perspectives*.

3. D. Bonhoeffer, *A Testament to Freedom*, p. 468.

4. Ibid., p. 475.

5. Ibid., p. 472.

6. Ibid., p. 499.

7. Hellmut Traub, "Two Recollections," in *I Knew Dietrich Bonhoeffer*, ed. Wolf-Dieter Zimmermann and Ronald Gregor Smith, p. 159.

8. D. Bonhoeffer, *A Testament to Freedom*, p. 479.

Chapter 15. Ethics

1. D. Bonhoeffer, *A Testament to Freedom*, p. 445.

2. Bethge, *Dietrich Bonhoeffer: A Biography*, p. 681.
3. Victoria Barnett, *For the Soul of the People: Protestant Protest Against Hitler,* p. 183.
4. D. Bonhoeffer, *A Testament to Freedom*, pp. 483–84.
5. Ibid., p. 485.
6. Geffrey B. Kelly, *Liberating Faith: Bonhoeffer's Message for Today,* p. 68.
7. Eberhard Bethge, *Bonhoeffer: Exile and Martyr*, p. 126.
8. D. Bonhoeffer, *Letters & Papers from Prison*, p. 163.
9. D. Bonhoeffer, *A Testament to Freedom*, p. 366.
10. D. Bonhoeffer, *Letters & Papers from Prison*, pp. 369–70.

Chapter 16. Deceptions for Peace

1. Bethge, *Bonhoeffer: Exile and Martyr*, p. 729.
2. Adolf Freudenberg, "Visits to Geneva," in *I Knew Dietrich Bonhoeffer*, ed. Wolf-Dieter Zimmermann and Ronald Gregor Smith, p. 169.
3. Leibholz-Bonhoeffer, *The Bonhoeffers: Portrait of a Family,* pp. 45–46.
4. Bethge, *Dietrich Bonhoeffer: A Biography*, pp. 762–63.

Chapter 17. Arrest

1. Robert Weldon Whalen, *Assassinating Hitler: Ethics and Resistance in Nazi Germany,* p. 141.
2. D. Bonhoeffer, *A Testament to Freedom*, p. 485.
3. Ibid., p. 427.
4. Bethge and others, *Dietrich Bonhoeffer: A Life in Pictures*, p. 207.
5. D. Bonhoeffer, *A Testament to Freedom*, p. 485.
6. Ibid., p. 501.
7. D. Bonhoeffer, *Letters & Papers from Prison*, p. 21.
8. Ibid., p. 22.

Chapter 18. Letters from Prison

1. Harald Poelchau, "The Freedom of the Prisoner," in *I Knew Dietrich Bonhoeffer*, ed. Wolf-Dieter Zimmermann and Ronald Gregor Smith, p. 222.
2. Bethge, *Dietrich Bonhoeffer: A Biography*, p. 814.
3. Ibid., p. 812.
4. Susanne Dress, "Meetings in Tegel," in *I Knew Dietrich Bonhoeffer*, ed. Wolf-Dieter Zimmermann and Ronald Gregor Smith, pp. 215–16.
5. Poelchau, "The Freedom of the Prisoner," in *I Knew Dietrich Bonhoeffer*, ed. Wolf-Dieter Zimmermann and Ronald Gregor Smith, pp. 222–23.
6. D. Bonhoeffer, *Letters & Papers from Prison*, p. 347.
7. Ibid., p. 279.
8. Ibid., p. 282.
9. Ibid., p. 347.
10. Ibid., p. 46.
11. Ibid., p. 162.
12. Ibid., p. 370.

13. Bethge, *Friendship and Resistance*, p. 44.

14. For a complete account of the Zossen Files, see Bethge, *Dietrich Bonhoeffer: A Biography*, Appendix 1, pp. 935–41.

15. D. Bonhoeffer, *Letters & Papers from Prison*, p. 393.

Chapter 19. The Last Days

1. D. Bonhoeffer, *A Testament to Freedom*, p. 522.

2. Fabian von Schlabrendorff, "In Prison with Dietrich Bonhoeffer," in *I Knew Dietrich Bonhoeffer*, ed. Wolf-Dieter Zimmermann and Ronald Gregor Smith, pp. 228–29.

3. Ibid., pp. 229–30.

4. Bosanquet, *Life and Death of Dietrich Bonhoeffer*, p. 271.

5. Bethge, *Dietrich Bonhoeffer: A Biography*, p. 927.

6. Ibid.

7. H. Fischer-Hüllstrung, "A Report from Fossenbürg," in *I Knew Dietrich Bonhoeffer*, ed. Wolf-Dieter Zimmermann and Ronald Gregor Smith, p. 232.

Chapter 20. Heritage of Faith

1. Leibholz-Bonhoeffer, *The Bonhoeffers: Portrait of a Family*, p. 164.

2. Bethge, *Dietrich Bonhoeffer: A Biography*, p. xiii.

3. Bethge, *Friendship and Resistance*, pp. 38–57.

4. Ibid., p. 56.

5. D. Bonhoeffer, *A Testament to Freedom*, p. 488.

6. Ruth-Alice von Bismarck and Ulrich Kabits, eds., *Love Letters from Cell 92: The Correspondence between Dietrich Bonhoeffer and Maria von Wedemeyer 1943–45*, p. 354.

7. Bethge, *Dietrich Bonhoeffer: A Biography*, p. xiv.

8. D. Bonhoeffer, *Letters & Papers from Prison*, p. 300.

9. Beatriz Melano, "The Influence of Dietrich Bonhoeffer, Paul Lehmann, and Richard Shaull in Latin America," *Princeton Seminary Bulletin* 22, no. 1 (2001): 83.

10. Chung Hyun Kyung, "Dear Dietrich Bonhoeffer: A Letter," in *Bonhoeffer for a New Day: Theology in a Time of Tradition*, ed. John W. De Gruchy, p. 10.

11. Victoria Barnett, "Dietrich Bonhoeffer's Ecumenical Vision," *Christian Century*, April 26, 1995, p. 454.

12. D. Bonhoeffer, *A Testament to Freedom*, p. 321.

13. Ibid., p. 508.

14. D. Bonhoeffer, *Letters & Papers from Prison*, p. 348.

Bibliography of
Sources Cited or Consulted

Bailey, J. Martin, and Douglas Gilbert. *The Steps of Bonhoeffer: A Pictorial Album*. Philadelphia: Pilgrim Press, 1969.

Barnes, Kenneth C. "Dietrich Bonhoeffer and Hitler's Persecution of the Jews." In *Betrayal: German Churches and the Holocaust*, edited by Robert P. Ericksen and Susannah Heschel, 110–27. Minneapolis: Fortress Press, 1999.

Barnett, Victoria J. "Dietrich Bonhoeffer's Ecumenical Vision." *Christian Century*, April 25, 1995, pp. 454–57.

———. *For the Soul of the People: Protestant Protest against Hitler*. New York: Oxford University Press, 1992.

Bentley, James. *Martin Niemöller: 1892–1984*. New York: Free Press, 1984.

Bergen, Doris L. *Twisted Cross: The German Christian Movement in the Third Reich*. Chapel Hill, N.C.: University of North Carolina Press, 1996.

Bethge, Eberhard. *Bonhoeffer: Exile and Martyr*. Edited by John W. De Gruchy. New York: Seabury Press, 1975.

———. *Dietrich Bonhoeffer: A Biography*. Revised and edited by Victoria J. Barnett. Minneapolis: Fortress Press, 2000.

———. *Dietrich Bonhoeffer: Man of Vision, Man of Courage*. Translated by Eric Mosbacher and others. New York: Harper & Row, 1967.

———. *Friendship and Resistance: Essays on Dietrich Bonhoeffer*. Grand Rapids, Mich.: William B. Eerdmans; Geneva: WCC Publications, 1995.

Bethge, Eberhard, and Renate Bethge, eds. *Last Letters of the Resistance:*

Farewells from the Bonhoeffer Family. Translated by Dennis Slabaugh. Philadelphia: Fortress Press, 1986.

Bethge, Eberhard, Renate Bethge, and Christian Gremmels, eds. *Dietrich Bonhoeffer: A Life in Pictures*. Translated by John Bowden. Philadelphia: Fortress Press, 1986.

Bismarck, Ruth-Alice von, and Ulrich Kabits, eds. *Love Letters from Cell 92: The Correspondence between Dietrich Bonhoeffer and Maria von Wedemeyer 1943–45*. Translated by John Brownjohn. Nashville, Tenn.: Abingdon, 1992.

Bonhoeffer, Dietrich. *The Cost of Discipleship*. First Touchstone Edition. New York: Simon & Schuster, 1995.

———. *Letters & Papers from Prison*. New Greatly Enlarged Edition, First Touchstone Edition. Edited by Eberhard Bethge. Translated by Reginald Fuller and others. New York: Simon & Schuster, 1997.

———. *No Rusty Swords: Letters, Lectures and Notes From the Collected Works of Dietrich Bonhoeffer, Vol. I*. Edited by Edwin H. Robertson. Translated by Edwin H. Robertson and John Bowden. New York: Harper & Row, 1965.

———. *A Testament to Freedom: The Essential Writings of Dietrich Bonhoeffer*. Rev. ed. Edited by Geffrey B. Kelly and F. Burton Nelson. San Francisco: Harper, 1995.

Bonhoeffer, Emmi. "Professors' Children as Neighbors." In *I Knew Dietrich Bonhoeffer: Reminiscences by His Friends*, edited by Wolf-Dieter Zimmermann and Ronald Gregor Smith, translated by Kathe Gregor Smith. New York: Harper & Row, 1964.

"Bonhoeffer Exonerated of Treason Charge." *Christian Century*, October 9, 1996, p. 929.

"Books of the Century: Leaders and Thinkers Weigh In On the Top 10." *Christianity Today*, April 24, 2000, pp. 92–93.

Bosanquet, Mary. *The Life and Death of Dietrich Bonhoeffer*. London: Hodder & Stoughton, 1968.

Brissaud, André. *Canaris: The Biography of Admiral Canaris, Chief of the German Military Intelligence in the Second World War*. Translated by Ian Colvin. New York: Grosset & Dunlap, 1974.

Burtness, James. *Shaping the Future: The Ethics of Dietrich Bonhoeffer*. Philadelphia: Fortress Press, 1985.

Chung Hyun Kyung. "Dear Dietrich Bonhoeffer." In *Bonhoeffer for a New Day: Theology in a Time of Tradition*, edited by John W. De Gruchy, 9–19. Grand Rapids, Mich.: William B. Eerdmans, 1997.

Cochrane, A. *The Church's Confession under Hitler*. Philadelphia: Westminster Press, 1962.

Conway, J. S. "The German Church Struggle: Its Making and Meaning." In
    The Church Confronts the Nazis, edited by Hubert G. Locke, 93–143. New
    York: E. Mellen Press, 1984.

Cresswell, Amos, and Maxwell Tow. *Dr. Franz Hildebrandt: Mr. Valliant-For-
    Truth.* Macon, Ga.: Smyth & Helwys, 2000.

De Gruchy, John W. *Bonhoeffer: Witness to Jesus Christ.* London: Collins, 1987.

———. *Bonhoeffer and South Africa: Theology in Dialogue.* Grand Rapids,
    Mich.: William B. Eerdmans, 1984.

———. "Bonhoeffer, Apartheid and Beyond: The Reception of Bonhoeffer in
    South Africa." In *Bonhoeffer for a New Day: Theology in a Time of Tradition,*
    edited by John W. De Gruchy, 353–65. Grand Rapids, Mich.: William B.
    Eerdmans, 1997.

———. *The Cambridge Companion to Dietrich Bonhoeffer.* Cambridge, U.K.:
    Cambridge University Press, 1999.

———. "Christian Witness in South Africa in a Time of Transition." In *The-
    ology and the Practice of Responsibility: Essays on Dietrich Bonhoeffer,* edited
    by Wayne Whitson Floyd, Jr., and Charles Marsh, 283–93. Valley Forge,
    Pa.: Trinity Press, 1994.

Detwiler, Donald S. *Germany: A Short History.* Carbondale, Ill.: Southern Illi-
    nois University Press, 1976.

Dietrich Bonhoeffer: Memories and Perspectives. Videocassette. Produced by
    Trinity Films, Inc., 1982. 90 min.

Dress, Susanne. "Meetings in Tegel." In *I Knew Dietrich Bonhoeffer: Reminis-
    cences by His Friends,* edited by Wolf-Dieter Zimmermann and Ronald
    Gregor Smith, translated by Kathe Gregor Smith. New York: Harper &
    Row, 1964.

Dudzus, Otto. "Arresting the Wheel." In *I Knew Dietrich Bonhoeffer: Reminis-
    cences by His Friends,* edited by Wolf-Dieter Zimmermann and Ronald
    Gregor Smith, translated by Kathe Gregor Smith. New York: Harper &
    Row, 1964.

Dumas, Andre. *Dietrich Bonhoeffer: Theologian of Reality.* Translated by Robert
    McAfee Brown. New York: Macmillan, 1968.

Fabricius, Cajus. *Positive Christianity in the Third Reich.* Hollywood, Calif.:
    New Christian Crusade Church, 1937.

Fest, Joachim. *Plotting Hitler's Death: The Story of the German Resistance.* New
    York: Henry Holt, 1994.

Fischer, Klaus P. *Nazi Germany: A New History.* New York: Continuum, 1995.

Floyd, Wayne Whitson, Jr. "Remembrance and Responsibility: Bonhoeffer's
    Many Faces." *Christian Century,* April 26, 1995, pp. 444–45.

Freudenberg, Adolf. "Visits to Geneva." In *I Knew Dietrich Bonhoeffer: Remi-*

niscences by His Friends, edited by Wolf-Dieter Zimmermann and Ronald Gregor Smith, translated by Kathe Gregor Smith. New York: Harper & Row, 1964.

Gerlach, Wolfgang. *And the Witnesses Were Silent: The Confessing Church and the Persecution of the Jews.* Translated and edited by Victoria J. Barnett. Lincoln, Neb.: University of Nebraska, 2000.

Gilbert, Martin. *The Day the War Ended: May 8, 1945—Victory in Europe.* New York: Henry Holt, 1995.

———. *The Holocaust: A History of the Jews of Europe During the Second World War.* New York: Henry Holt, 1987.

Glazener, Mary. *The Cup of Wrath.* Savannah, Ga: F. C. Bell, 1992.

Godsey, John D. "Bonhoeffer and the Third World: West Africa, Cuba, Korea." In *Ethical Responsibility: Bonhoeffer's Legacy to the Churches,* edited by John D. Godsey and Geffrey B. Kelly, 257–65. New York: Edwin Mellen Press, 1981.

Godsey, John D., and Geffrey B. Kelly, eds. *Ethical Responsibility: Bonhoeffer's Legacy to the Churches.* New York: Edwin Mellen Press, 1981.

Goebel, Johannes. "When He Sat Down at the Piano." In *I Knew Dietrich Bonhoeffer: Reminiscences by His Friends,* edited by Wolf-Dieter Zimmermann and Ronald Gregor Smith, translated by Kathe Gregor Smith. New York: Harper & Row, 1964.

Gollwitzer, Helmut, and others, eds. *Dying We Live: The Final Messages and Records of the Resistance.* New York: Pantheon, 1956.

Gosser, Jonathan P., and Robin W. Lovin. "An Encounter with Eberhard Bethge." *Christian Century,* March 31, 1976, pp. 313–14.

Green, Clifford J. *Bonhoeffer: A Theology of Sociality.* Rev. ed. Grand Rapids, Mich.: William B. Eerdmans, 1999.

Grunfeld, Frederic V. *The Hitler File: A Social History of Germany and the Nazis 1918–45.* New York: Random House, 1974.

Hamerow, Theodore S. *On the Road to the Wolf's Lair: German Resistance to Hitler.* Cambridge, Mass.: Belknap Press, 1997.

Helmreich, Ernst Christian. *The German Churches under Hitler: Background, Struggle, and Epilogue.* Detroit: Wayne State University Press, 1979.

Herman, Stewart W. *It's Your Souls We Want.* New York: Harper & Brothers, 1943.

———. *The Rebirth of the German Church.* New York: Harper & Brothers, 1946.

Hildebrandt, Franz. "An Oasis of Freedom." In *I Knew Dietrich Bonhoeffer: Reminiscences by His Friends,* edited by Wolf-Dieter Zimmermann and Ronald Gregor Smith, translated by Kathe Gregor Smith. New York: Harper & Row, 1964.

Hoffmann, Peter. *German Resistance to Hitler*. Cambridge, Mass.: Harvard
    University Press, 1988.

———. *The History of the German Resistance 1933–1945*. Translated by Richard
    Barry. Cambridge, Mass.: MIT Press, 1977.

Höhne, Heinz. *Canaris*. Translated by J. Maxwell Brownjohn. New York:
    Doubleday, 1979.

Jensen, Hans-Werner. "Life Together." In *I Knew Dietrich Bonhoeffer: Reminis-
    cences by His Friends,* edited by Wolf-Dieter Zimmermann and Ronald
    Gregor Smith, translated by Kathe Gregor Smith. New York: Harper &
    Row, 1964.

Jiebuhr, Gustav. "Undoing the Legacy of the Nazi Courts." *New York Times,*
    February 11, 1997, Section 4, p. 6.

Kelly, Geffrey B. *Liberating Faith: Bonhoeffer's Message for Today.* Minneapolis:
    Augsburg, 1984.

Kinzer, Stephen. "New Effort to Clear an Anti-Nazi Martyr Still Branded a
    Traitor." *New York Times*, February 5, 1996, A7.

Kitchen, Martin. *Nazi Germany at War*. New York: Longman, 1995.

Koch, Werner. "Dietrich Bonhoeffer in Pomerania." In *I Knew Dietrich Bon-
    hoeffer: Reminiscences by His Friends*, edited by Wolf-Dieter Zimmer-
    mann and Ronald Gregor Smith, translated by Kathe Gregor Smith.
    New York: Harper & Row, 1964.

Lang, Jochen von. *Adolf Hitler: Faces of a Dictator*. New York: Harcourt, Brace
    & World, Inc., 1968.

Leibholz-Bonhoeffer, Sabine. *The Bonhoeffers: Portrait of a Family*. Chicago:
    Covenant, 1994.

Maltusch, Gottfried. "When the Synagogues Burnt." In *I Knew Dietrich Bon-
    hoeffer: Reminiscences by His Friends*, edited by Wolf-Dieter Zimmer-
    mann and Ronald Gregor Smith, translated by Kathe Gregor Smith.
    New York: Harper & Row, 1964.

Marle, Rene. *Bonhoeffer: The Man and His Work*. New York: Newman, 1967.

Meding, Dorothee von. *Courageous Hearts: Women and the Anti-Hitler Plot of
    1944*. Providence: Berghahn Books, 1997.

Melano, Beatriz. "The Influence of Dietrich Bonhoeffer, Paul Lehmann, and
    Richard Shaull in Latin America." *Princeton Seminary Bulletin* 22, no. 1
    (2001): 64–84.

Paulsell, William O. *Tough Minds, Tender Hearts*. New York: Paulist Press,
    1990.

Poelchau, Harald. "The Freedom of the Prisoner." In *I Knew Dietrich Bon-
    hoeffer: Reminiscences by His Friends*, edited by Wolf-Dieter Zimmer-

mann and Ronald Gregor Smith, translated by Kathe Gregor Smith. New York: Harper & Row, 1964.

Rasmussen, Larry. *Dietrich Bonhoeffer—His Significance for North Americans.* Minneapolis: Fortress Press, 1990.

Robertson, E. H. *Dietrich Bonhoeffer.* Atlanta, Ga.: John Knox Press, 1976.

Robertson, Edwin. *The Shame and the Sacrifice: The Life and Martyrdom of Dietrich Bonhoeffer.* New York: Macmillan, 1988.

Rose, Jonathan, ed. *The Holocaust and the Book: Destruction and Preservation.* Amherst, Mass.: University of Massachusetts, 2001.

Rother, Richard. "A Confirmation Class in Wedding." In *I Knew Dietrich Bonhoeffer: Reminiscences by His Friends,* edited by Wolf-Dieter Zimmermann and Ronald Gregor Smith, translated by Kathe Gregor Smith. New York: Harper & Row, 1964.

Schlabrendorff, Fabian von. "In Prison with Dietrich Bonhoeffer." In *I Knew Dietrich Bonhoeffer: Reminiscences by His Friends,* edited by Wolf-Dieter Zimmermann and Ronald Gregor Smith, translated by Kathe Gregor Smith. New York: Harper & Row, 1964.

Scholder, Klaus. *The Churches and the Third Reich, Vols. I and II.* Translated by John Bowden. Philadelphia: Fortress Press, 1977.

———. *A Requiem for Hitler and Other New Perspectives on the German Church Struggle.* Translated by John Bowden. London: Trinity Press, 1989.

Smith, Ronald Gregor, ed. *World Come of Age.* Philadelphia: Fortress Press, 1967.

Spielvogel, Jackson J. *Hitler and Nazi Germany: A History.* 4th ed. Upper Saddle River, N.J.: Prentice Hall, 2001.

Thomsett, Michael C. *The German Opposition to Hitler: The Resistance, the Underground, and Assassination Plots, 1938–1945.* Jefferson, N.C.: McFarland, 1997.

Traub, Hellmut. "Two Recollections." In *I Knew Dietrich Bonhoeffer: Reminiscences by His Friends,* edited by Wolf-Dieter Zimmermann and Ronald Gregor Smith, translated by Kathe Gregor Smith. New York: Harper & Row, 1964.

Vexler, Robert, ed. *Germany: A Chronology and Fact Book 1415–1972.* Dobbs Ferry, N.Y.: Oceana, 1973.

Vorkink, Peter, II., ed. *Bonhoeffer in a World Come of Age.* Philadelphia: Fortress Press, 1968.

Whalen, Robert Weldon. *Assassinating Hitler: Ethics and Resistance in Nazi Germany.* Selinsgrove, Pa.: Susquehanna University Press, 1993.

Wind, Renate. *Dietrich Bonhoeffer: A Spoke in the Wheel.* Translated by John Bowden. Grand Rapids, Mich.: William B. Eerdmans, 1992.

Wise, Stephen A. "Why Isn't Bonhoeffer Honored at Yad Vashem?" *Christianity Today,* February 25, 1998, pp. 202–4.

Wolf, Ernst. "Political and Moral Motives behind the Resistance." In *The German Resistance to Hitler.* Berkeley: University of California Press, 1970.

Zimmermann, Wolf-Dieter, and Ronald Gregor Smith, eds. *I Knew Dietrich Bonhoeffer: Reminiscences by His Friends.* Translated by Kathe Gregor Smith. New York: Harper & Row, 1964.

Zentner, Christian, and Friedemann Bedürftig, eds. *The Encyclopedia of the Third Reich.* New York: Macmillan, 1991.

Conversations with the Author

Bethge, Eberhard. Villiprot, Germany. July 10, 1998.
Bethge, Renate. Villiprot, Germany. July 10, 1998.
Bismarck, Ruth-Alice von. Hamburg, Germany. July 15, 1998.
Bracher, Dorothee. Villiprot, Germany. July 10, 1998.
Hase, Hans-Christoph von. Kassel, Germany. July 12, 1998.
Zimmermann, Wolf-Dieter. Berlin, Germany. July 21, 1998.

Index

Thomas Merton and Thich Nhat Hanh:
Engaged Spirituality in an Age of Globalization

ROBERT H. KING

"*Thomas Merton and Thich Nhat Hanh* is a timely in-depth look at how Merton and Hanh, Christian and Buddhist, successfully integrated their spiritual and political lives. King uses his considerable analytical and research abilities to create a work that is comprehensive and insightful as well as personal and global in its conclusions. Using their writings and journals, and King's own sense of the urgency of their message, he not only illustrates how these two men recreated their religions in ways that that allowed their spiritual practice to become the foundation for political action in the world, but also how they were able to find in each other's religion new depths in their own."

—*Springs Magazine*

OTHER BOOKS PUBLISHED BY CONTINUUM

The Spiritual Legacy of Thomas Merton

DEIRDRE LaNOUE

"What this biography does is inform you 'about' Henri Nouwen, effectively putting all the pieces together, linking what was happening in his personal life with his maturing faith and what books he was writing at the time. The result is a well-researched revelation of his North American odyssey from marching in Selma to working with L'Arche, a community that cares for the disabled. But this is more than a biography. Ms. LaNoue . . . goes deeper. She draws from Father Nouwen's literary work one overall message. She finds a spiritual guide whose uniqueness lay in bringing two ancient Christian concepts—that God loves you and that the path to spiritual maturity lies in detachment from the 'busyness'—to the use of psychology."

—*The Dallas Morning News*

Befriending the Beloved Disciple:
A Jewish Reading of the Gospel of John

ADELE REINHARTZ

"Adele Reinhartz's long-awaited and elegantly written book enriches our knowledge of emerging Judaism and Christianity. *Befriending the Beloved Disciple* engages in a very generous and original reading of the Fourth Gospel from a critical but sympathetic Jewish perspective. This is 'must' reading for anyone concerned with the long history of anti-Judaism engendered by the Christian Gospels. I highly recommend it."

—Elisabeth Schüssler Fiorenza,
Harvard Divinity School

"*Befriending the Beloved Disciple* is an invigorating exercise in situated reading. Adele Reinhartz candidly lays out her reader's position in relation to John's Gospel as a Jew and a feminist, and then instructively explores the ways in which a reader so situated might relate to this text that insistently demands of its audience adherence to a particular community of belief. There is much to be learned here both about John and about the reading process."

—Robert Alter,
The University of California, Berkeley

OTHER BOOKS PUBLISHED BY CONTINUUM

Beyond Fear and Silence:
A Feminist-Literary Reading of Mark

JOAN L. MITCHELL

"In this contribution to feminist biblical studies, Joan Mitchell shows how an informed reading and hearing of familiar scriptural stories can lead to a new understanding of women's importance as faithful followers of Jesus and especially as significant eye-witnesses at the empty tomb on Easter morning. In the silence of the women at the tomb (Mk 16:8), Mitchell insists, Mark calls the disciples of future generations 'to speak for themselves and bring the gospel into dialogue with their lives.' School and college teachers interested in including a feminist perspective in their scripture courses will definitely place this high on their list of required readings."

—Catherine McNamee,
Former President,
National Catholic Educational Association